contents

foreword by Dr Dorothy Einon

Learning should be fun. Preschool children do not make any distinction between work and play or between playing and learning. All learning is embraced with enthusiasm as long as a child enjoys what he is doing.

Children learn about the world through play, but they don't always know how to organize or direct their play. This is why your child needs you to participate. All the games, tasks and activities in this book are designed for you and your child to do together. The learning may be serious, but the games are lighthearted – keep them that way. Talk, laugh and gossip as you play together, and offer guidance when it's needed.

Children tend to learn more effectively if they are allowed to run around and let off steam before they sit still to concentrate on a task. I've found that the best way to do this is to put on some music and let children run around, shout and dance until the music stops. Young children, and boys in particular, find it difficult to sit still for long periods. One of the benefits of running around is that it gets blood pumping round the body, which brings a plentiful supply of oxygen to the brain.

You are the best judge of how long it is reasonable to expect your child to concentrate on a task. In my experience, an hour is a very long time for most three-year-olds. If you notice signs that your child is losing interest, fidgeting or becoming distracted, it may be time to stop.

Another good way of preparing for 'serious play' is to clear away any toys or other

Above: Children's love of water means that they will be naturally drawn to a water-based activity.

Right: Role-play creates an ideal environment for combining enjoyment with mental stimulation.

Left: Using familiar objects like bricks makes learning much more fun.

Below: An activity such as making a cake stimulates a child on many levels.

distractions that don't relate to the activity you're about to do. Small children are easily distracted and if there are competing activities they may find it hard to concentrate on the immediate task, particularly if it is a demanding one that requires a lot of thought. For this reason, it's also a good idea to turn off the radio or television.

One of the biggest aids to learning in children is self belief. It is amazing what children can achieve when they believe in their own competence and capabilities. This is why it's very important to praise a child for effort and make a fuss of success. Criticism undermines small children, damages their self-confidence and, ultimately, makes them feel that it is safer not to attempt something if they risk failure.

If your child starts misbehaving or being silly during an activity, rather than getting angry with him or telling him off, try saying: 'I can see you are not enjoying this – let's put it away for another day'. Putting pressure on your child to continue with something that doesn't interest him is counterproductive – research suggests

that young children who are pushed too hard, either in school or at home, often underachieve.

If your child habitually fidgets or misbehaves, you may need to practise sitting still and concentrating. Playing at the sink, reading stories, looking at books or sitting down with a drink and a biscuit for a chat are all good ways of doing this.

If your child struggles or responds badly to a particular activity, stop it and try an easier one. Look through the chapters in this book and find a game or activity that you think your child will enjoy. For example, he may not count building bricks but he may count toy cars. If your child is allowed to succeed at one activity he will be motivated to try other more difficult tasks. He should always feel that he has succeeded more often than he has failed.

Where possible, adapt a task or an activity to your child's interests and preferences. For example, if he won't sit still and draw shapes on paper, he might ride his bike around shapes drawn in water or chalk in a playground. Let the games stimulate your imagination too.

words

and music

introduction

Normal, loving and responsive care-giving is fundamental to helping your child fulfil her intellectual potential. Once this is in place, however, one form of stimulation that has been proven to make a real difference is language.

You can raise your child's IQ simply by engaging her in lots of conversation, encouraging her responses and enjoying each other's company. Because language is the main avenue to learning about the world, it is likely that just talking and listening to your child is the most important form of intellectual stimulation she will ever receive.

Music is another form of stimulation that has been shown to boost brain development. The processing of musical sounds is closely related to the processing of speech sounds: both activate similar brain regions, suggesting that music is a sort of pre-linguistic language. The ability to listen is a prerequisite to analysing both speech and musical sounds.

The language, music and listening games in this section should primarily be done for fun. It is not the intention to 'push' or pressurize your child, but to enhance her development through shared activities that are enjoyable for both of you.

Language

Between the ages of 7 and 12 months, the sound of a baby's babbling begins to change subtly. More consonant sounds will be creeping in, and by 12 months a baby may speak her first word – a thrilling moment for every parent. Although the age at which this happens is not related to subsequent language development, a child's vocabulary at

3 years does predict what their vocabulary will be like as an adult.

Research shows that during the first 3 years of a child's life, when brain growth is at its peak, parents can make a tremendous difference to their child's subsequent vocabulary and IQ. Three factors count: the quantity of language that is spoken directly to the child (not just overheard by the child), the quality of language the child hears (for example, the number of descriptive words, less common words, word explanations), and the parents' style of interacting with the child (that is, how responsive, positive and encouraging they are).

Music

The main characteristics of music – pitch, timbre, intensity and rhythm – are all found in spoken language. For this reason, musical experience can help a child listen to, remember, integrate and produce language sounds. In the same way that a baby plays with speech sounds while babbling, repeated tunes, songs and nursery rhymes are seen as games by young children – as 'toys' for the ear and voice.

Apart from the effects of music on language development, exposing your child to musical activities or instruction can result in many other benefits including a higher IQ, enhanced abstract reasoning ability, improved auditory memory, increased creativity and better manual dexterity.

Listening

Skilled listening requires a child to concentrate on selected sounds. Listening ability is the starting point for a vast amount of learning, whether through exposure to language or to all kinds of music.

The talking, listening, rhyming, singing, reading, finger-play, music and movement games in this section are designed to help accelerate the 'wiring up' of language, music and listening circuits in the brain – all of which are essential to the full realization of your child's intellectual potential.

all about me

Games to help your child learn about body parts.

Teaching your child the names of the different parts of the body can be great fun, and the games here include lots of hands-on contact and tickling. By linking actions such as clapping and nodding with the parts of his body and by making the games and action songs stimulating and enjoyable, you will improve your child's co-ordination and mental acuity.

bath action
from 18 months

This game focuses on the names of body parts as well as some interesting action words (verbs).

- Make your toddler's bath toys perform and encourage her to tell you what each one is doing.

- Pick up the fish and say 'Oh look! The fish is diving, diving, diving under your leg! What is it doing?' Make it dive several times under your toddler's leg and see if she can tell you 'It is diving'.

- Then pick up the soap and say 'Oh look! The soap is washing, washing, washing your hands. What is it doing?'

- Continue with other objects, linking their actions with your child's body parts. For example: the boat is zooming, zooming, zooming past your tummy; the frog is splashing, splashing, splashing on your back, and so on.

RESEARCH SAYS

' The repetition of words and phrases is one of the best ways to accelerate your child's language development. It helps to reinforce the neural pathways in her brain that link sound with meaning. '

bear, bee & tabby cat

from 2 years

Repeating favourite hand and finger games helps your child recognize familiar words and phrases.

- Ask your toddler to hold out her hand, palm upwards. Gently draw a circle round and round on her palm with your finger, saying 'Round and round the garden, like a teddy bear...'

- 'Walk' your fingers slowly up her arm, saying 'One step, two steps...' Then, as you say 'And tickle you under there!' tickle her under her arm.

- Now try: 'Round and round the garden, like a bumblebee... One flight, two flights (make your hand take two pouncing 'flights' up her arm)... And a tickle from me!'

- Go back to the original version, but substitute 'tabby cat' for 'teddy bear', and finish with 'And tickle you like that!'

in & out

from 2 years

Linking words with actions will help to extend vocabulary and concentration skills.

- Stand facing your child. Put your hand out in front of you, then behind, as you say 'Put this hand in, take this hand out, put this hand in, now shake it all about.' See if she can copy your actions and words.

- Now try: 'Put your fingers in your ears, pull your fingers out...', 'Put this leg in, take this leg out...', 'Put that arm in, take that arm out...'. Shake the body part each time.

- Later you can teach 'up' and 'down' and 'under' and 'over', matching your words with appropriate actions.

the toe family
from 18 months

- Sit your toddler on your lap, hold her big toe and ask 'What toe is this?' Pause, then say 'This is great big daddy toe. He can stretch!' Gently pull her toe.

- Move to the next toe, asking 'What toe is this?' Pause, then say 'This is mummy toe. She can bend!' Gently bend the toe.

- Continue with 'brother toe', saying 'He can throw and catch!' Bend this toe gently back and forth.

- Next comes 'sister toe' and 'She can giggle!' Shake this toe a little.

- Finish with 'baby toe', who 'likes to wiggle and jiggle all the way home!' Jiggle this toe, and tickle and bounce your child on your knee. With time, see if she can supply the name of each toe.

Playing this game will help your toddler learn the names of family members and some interesting actions.

two things at once
from 2 years

This game is an excellent way to boost your toddler's listening and verbal memory skills, while improving balance and co-ordination.

- Ask your toddler 'Can you touch your nose like this?' Put one finger on the end of your nose and see if she can copy you. Say 'Well done!' and keep your finger on your nose.

- Now say 'Can you touch your ear like this at the same time?' Move on to other double pointing actions: cheek and chin, tummy and neck, ankle and toe, and so on.

- Always give one instruction at a time. Make sure she can point to one body part before adding a second.

what are these for?

AA

from 2 years

- Hold up both hands, asking 'What are these for? Hands are for folding.' (Fold hands together.) 'And for clapping – clap, clap!' (Clap twice.) Encourage your child to copy your words and actions.

- Show your toes, asking 'What are these for? Toes are for pointing.' (Point to toes.) 'And tapping – tap! tap!' (Tap toes twice.)

- Point to both eyes, asking 'What are these for? Eyes are for sleeping.' (Close eyes.) 'And looking – yes, boo!' (Open eyes wide.)

- Point to your nose, asking 'But what is this for? A nose is for sniffing.' (Sniff.) 'And sneezing – ah-choo!' (Pretend to sneeze.)

This action rhyme is a fun way to expand your child's vocabulary and teach her what certain body parts are useful for.

RESEARCH SAYS

6 **Between the ages of 1 and 3 years, the average number of words parents address directly to their children each hour varies from as little as 600 to more than 2,000. The more words children hear, the better their vocabulary and IQ scores.** 9

AA chinny chin-chin

from 18 months

Alliteration appeals to children of this age. This game will draw your toddler's attention to various speech sounds and encourage her to try using them herself.

- Face your toddler, point to her chin and say 'Oh look! Here's your... (pause) ... chinny chin-chin!' Emphasize the 'ch' sound and rub your chins together.

- Ask 'What is it?' Pause, encouraging your child to answer with you: 'It's your... chinny chin-chin.'

- Now point to your child's cheek and say 'Oh look! Here's your cheeky cheek-cheek!' Rub cheeks together and ask 'What is it? It's your... cheeky cheek-cheek.'

- Continue with other body parts: lippy lip-lips, nosey nose-nose, handy hand-hand and so on.

RESEARCH SAYS

❝ The best way to enhance your toddler's language development is to have lots of one-on-one conversations, where you take turns listening and responding to each other. ❞

my turn, your turn

from 18 months

Games where you and your toddler take turns, as in conversation, are an ideal way to boost her language abilities.

- Sit facing your child and say 'Look! Here's mummy's (daddy's) tummy!'

- Touch your stomach and ask 'Do you have a tummy? Where's your tummy?' Help your child to find, and point to, her tummy.

- Point to her tummy and ask (as if you've forgotten already) 'What's this again?' This gives your child a chance to name the body part herself.

- Continue in this way with other body parts.

where oh where?

from 18 months

Your toddler loves hiding games and this one is an excellent way to introduce her to the names of different body parts.

- Cover your head with a cloth and say 'Where oh where is mummy's (daddy's) *head*?', emphasizing the word 'head'. If your toddler doesn't immediately pull the cloth off, encourage her by shaking your head a little.

- Once she has found your head, exclaim 'Oh yes, here's my *head*!' as you point to it.

- Now cover other body parts and see if your toddler can find them.

fee fie foe opposites

from 2 years

- Begin with 'Fee fie foe fum, oh here it is, here's mummy's (daddy's) *great big* thumb!' Emphasize the adjectives 'great big' and hold up your thumb.

- Repeat this rhyme together so that your child has a chance to use these words herself.

- Now say 'Fee fie foe fum, where is (your child's name)'s *tiny little* thumb?' Emphasize the words 'tiny little'. Your child should now hold up her thumb for comparison. Then repeat the rhyme together.

- Once your toddler is familiar with the concepts of 'great big' and 'tiny little', introduce other opposites such as fat and thin, short and tall, large and small.

This game is similar to Fee Fie Foe Fum! (see opposite), but includes adjectives describing size. Children learn to use these later than many other adjectives.

finer fee fie foe

from 2 years

Expand your child's vocabulary and observational skills by focusing on the finer descriptive details of different people's body parts.

- Sit facing your toddler and say 'Fee fie foe fum, here's (your child's name)'s... dusty knee.' Use an appropriate adjective: grazed, bent, straight, chubby and so on.

- Repeat this rhyme together so that your child has a chance to use the new adjective.

- Now say 'Fee fie foe fum, here's mummy's (daddy's) knee. What does it look like?' Discuss its appearance in as much detail as possible.

- Continue with other body parts, helping your child to notice how the details differ for each of you.

fee fie foe fum!

A A **from 2 years**

- Sit in a comfortable position with your child. Say 'Fee fie foe *fum*, oh here it is, here's mummy's (daddy's) thumb!' Hold up your thumb for her to see.

- Now say 'Fee fie foe *fum*, oh here it is, here's (your child's name)'s thumb!' Hold up your child's thumb for display.

- Continue in this way for other body parts, changing the word 'fum' to rhyme with each part: 'Fee fie foe *fears*, oh here they are, here are _____'s ears!', or 'Fee fie foe *farm*, oh here it is, here's _____'s arm!'

Learning the names of different body parts is fun and will help your child connect new words with their meaning.

RESEARCH SAYS

❝ Children whose parents use a wide variety of nouns, adjectives and verbs during conversation with them from birth to age 2 years end up with better vocabularies and higher verbal IQ scores. ❞

♫ where do these go?

from 18 months

This singing game will enhance your toddler's logical thinking skills and boost his vocabulary.

● Play this game when you are helping your toddler get dressed in the morning, during the day, or at bedtime.

● Give your child a choice. Say 'Here are your socks. I wonder where these go?' Sing to the tune of *Do You Know the Muffin Man*: 'Do these go on your ears or feet, your ears or feet, your ears or feet?' Praise your toddler for the right answer.

● Ask similar questions, by singing, as you help your child put on each item of clothing.

RESEARCH SAYS

' Children aged 4 and 5 years were taught the names of body parts through instructional songs with movements. After 20 days' teaching, their vocabulary and creativity scores were substantially higher than those of children taught by either verbal instruction, or verbal instruction with movements. '

♫ simple simon says

from 2 years

Accelerate the development of your child's creativity and language abilities with this singing and action game.

- Stand in front of your toddler and give instructions to the tune of *Baa, Baa, Black Sheep*, as follows: 'Simple Simon (Sally) says wave your arm like this, wave your arm like this, wave your arm like this!' Show your child how to wave one arm and encourage him to sing.

- Continue with further commands such as kick your leg, nod your head, march up and down, each time acting out your words for your child to copy.

- Later, switch roles so that your child gives the orders and you follow them.

♫ stanley the statue

from 2 years

Singing commands will help your child learn vocabulary related to body parts very rapidly.

- Tell your child that you are Stanley (Stella) the statue. Stand very still and explain that statues don't move.

- Say 'I can't move, but see if you can do what I tell you. Listen very carefully. Are you ready?'

- Sing to the tune of *The Wheels on The Bus*: 'Stanley (Stella) the statue says touch your ears, touch your ears, touch your ears!' See if your child can follow this command. If not, show him how.

- Continue by singing commands to touch other body parts, being careful not to move yourself. Encourage your child to join in with the singing.

what colour?

from 18 months

This choosing game will help your child learn colour names and improve her observation and thinking skills.

RESEARCH SAYS

‘ Categorization – grouping things by their similarities and differences – is one of the main ways children learn new words. ’

- Draw your child's attention to the colours of everyday objects as you encounter them: a red block, a blue shirt, a yellow banana, a green leaf, a brown teapot.

- Then, focus her attention on the colours of various body parts and items of clothing.

- Ask her questions such as 'These are my teeth (point to them); what colour are they?' If she is unable to answer, give her a choice of two – 'Green or white?'

- Continue in this way with other body parts, then move on to clothing: 'On your hands you have some mittens. What colour are they? Pink or blue?'

same or different?

AA **from 18 months**

This game teaches your toddler the concepts of 'same' and 'different', while reinforcing her knowledge of the names of body parts.

- Collect a few of your child's favourite toy animals in a basket and cover with a cloth.

- Now point to your ear and ask 'What's this? This is my _____?' Encourage your toddler to answer.

- Ask her to choose a toy. Then ask 'Is (teddy, say) the *same* as I am – does he have an ear?' Emphasize the word 'same'.

- Have your toddler locate one of teddy's ears, then exclaim 'So teddy *is* the same as I am. He *does* have an ear!'

- Continue in this way with other body parts and toys.

one or two?

AA **from 2 years**

Help your child to develop an understanding of the numbers 'one' and 'two', while reinforcing her vocabulary.

- Ask your child 'How many hands do you have? One or two?'

- Then help her count her hands: 'One... two!' Ask her how many hands you have: 'One or two?' Again, help her count.

- Mix up your questions so that sometimes the answer is 'one' and sometimes 'two'. For example: 'How many necks do you have, one or two?'

- Later, draw attention to the body parts of animals. Ask silly questions to challenge her thinking, for example: 'How many wings do you have, one or two?'

what can you do?

from 2 years

- Point to your child's eyes and ask 'What can you do with these? Can you blink them?'

- Now ask your child to point to some part of your body and ask you 'What can you do with that?' If she points to an arm, for example, you might answer 'With my arm, I can wave.' Then wave your arm.

- Next, point to your child's feet and ask 'What can you do with these?' You may need to encourage her by saying 'What are they? Can you jump with your feet?'

- Your child then points to another part of your body and asks 'What can you do with that?' Continue taking turns in this way.

Give your child an opportunity to take charge and make decisions. It will boost her creative thinking as well.

head, arms & legs

from 2 years

Designed to help improve your child's vocabulary, this game also boosts her creative thinking.

- Ask your child 'What can you do with your head? I can shake my head from side to side (shake your head). What can you do with your head?' Encourage her to show you something different she can do with her head and help her describe what she is doing.

- Then ask 'Can you do something else with your head? I can stretch my head way back like this. Can you think of something different you can do with your head?'

- Continue to take turns until neither of you can think of anything else you can do with your head. Move on to your arms, and then your legs.

A A nose & toes

from 2 years

- Face your child and ask 'Can you do what I do?'

- Use both hands to touch your nose, asking 'Can you touch your nose?' Praise your toddler when she copies you.

- Now ask 'Can you touch your toes?' Use both hands to touch your toes.

- Say 'Good! Now can you touch your nose and then toes?' Touch your nose first, then your toes, for your child to copy.

- Move on to other pairs of body parts. Speak quite slowly to begin with.

- When your child becomes good at this, graduate to three body parts. For example: 'Can you touch your tummy, knees and toes?'

This game will enhance your toddler's co-ordination and balance, and her ability to remember what she hears.

RESEARCH SAYS

In one study, babies whose parents followed a programme of early activities designed to stimulate language development began to say their first words between 7 and 9 months of age. By 10 months, some were uttering simple sentences.

things I do

Games to teach your child about daily routines.

Making games out of everyday chores will help your child to learn about daily life in a fun and innovative way. From memorizing what is needed from the shops to sorting laundry by colour or learning to dress herself, your child's memory and language skills will improve. She will also become accustomed to daily routines, which can reinforce her feelings of security.

book projects
from 18 months

Reading books to your toddler and talking about them together will have a significant impact on her many developing abilities.

RESEARCH SAYS

' As soon as a toddler can say about 50 words, her vocabulary begins to explode. On average, this milestone is reached around 18 months. '

- Try to read to your toddler every day. Books with lift-up flaps or other features that invite her interaction are ideal. Books about mother and baby, everyday activities, animals or with a repetitive storyline appeal to children of this age.

- Try to include sound effects and strange voices in your reading.

- After reading a book, suggest that you both look back through it to find various people, animals or objects: 'Let's look again to find that monkey (cake, baby, bottle, crocodile, puppy...).' Exclaim in triumph as each search is successful. Encourage your child to suggest things she wants to look for.

- As each is found, repeat the name several times and remind your child what is happening in the picture.

shopping
from 2 years

This game helps your child learn about a sequence of events, as well as words that signal the passing of time.

- Pretending to put on your coat, sing to the tune of *London Bridge is Falling Down*: 'Let's go and do the shopping now, shopping now, shopping now, Let's go and do the shopping now, my fair (child's name) – oh!'

- Repeat this pattern of words, with changes to words and actions:

- 'First we find a shopping cart (x3), my fair...' (Collect a wagon, basket or bag.)
  'Now we put the goodies in (x3), my fair...'
  'Next we go to the checkout tills (x3), my fair...'
  'We get some bags and load them up (x3), my fair...'
  'Then we take the groceries home (x3), my fair...'
  'Now we put the food away (x3), my fair...'
  'We've finished all the shopping now (x3), Well done! _____ – oh!'

sorting sorties
from 18 months

Sorting games will improve your toddler's vocabulary, as well as her visual and verbal memory.

- Encourage your child to help you sort clothes into piles (socks, underwear, tops, towels...), or into the appropriate drawers and cupboards, or into groups according to which family member they belong to.

- Together, sort toys into containers or locations. Sort cutlery into compartmentalized trays; sort laundry for the washing machine into white, light-coloured and dark-coloured piles.

- Encourage your toddler to help you sort shoes or socks into pairs and crayons or balls by colour.

♫ good morning!
from 18 months

- Ask your child 'What do we do in the morning?'

- Then sing this song to the tune of *Mary Had a Little Lamb*, encouraging her to join in with the words and actions: 'In the morning, we wake up and stretch, wake up and stretch, wake up and stretch! In the morning we wake up and stretch. Oh, yes we do.' (Lie down, open eyes, yawn and stretch.)

- Ask your child what happens next and then sing another verse based on this. For example: 'We go to the bathroom and wash our faces; we look for our clothes and put them on; we go to the kitchen and eat some breakfast; we go to the bathroom and brush our teeth.' Match the words to your toddler's morning routine.

This game will help develop your toddler's understanding of how events are sequenced in time.

1, 2, 3, feed me!
from 18 months

Mealtimes provide a perfect opportunity to develop your toddler's number concepts.

- Cut up your child's food into bite-sized pieces and help her count them.

- Say 'Oh look, it's some banana! How many pieces? Let's count!' Hold her hand, help her point, and count together: 'One! Two!'

- Ask again how many pieces, and count again. Then count each piece as your toddler eats them.

- Start this game by offering just one, two or three pieces each time. Gradually introduce four, five and six.

AA concept matching
from 18 months

- **Size** Encourage your child to find pictures of animals or objects in books that are different sizes: large ('big, huge, gigantic, giant-sized'), average ('middle-sized'), and small ('little, tiny, minute'). Use the same terms to describe items encountered in real life. Plastic cups and spoons, cooking pots with lids and painted wooden Russian dolls are useful for this.

- **Colours** Play a book game where you say 'There is something green (blue, red, yellow...) on this page. Can you find it?' Also use colour words to describe things during the day: useful toys include building blocks, stacking cups and crayons.

Help your toddler develop concepts of size and colour by matching what she sees in books with everyday objects.

RESEARCH SAYS

'A toddler of 18 months may say only 50 or so words, but she will understand three or four times as many. Between the ages of 2 and 6 years, children learn the meaning of an amazing eight new words per day!'

artist at work
from 18 months

Drawing and painting are excellent ways to boost your child's vocabulary, fine motor skills and creative talents.

- Provide your toddler with suitable drawing and painting materials, different-coloured papers and perhaps a black- or whiteboard.

- Use her random artistic ventures to develop her language skills. Comment and ask questions about the colours, shapes, patterns, and drawing or painting techniques she uses.

- Help your child count the colours she used in her picture, or the number of times she drew wavy, curved or straight lines.

- Compare some of the shapes she produces to known objects: 'That round circle looks like someone's head (a ball, plate, apple...).'

RESEARCH SAYS

' The amount of language a child hears makes a tremendous difference to her vocabulary and verbal IQ, but it is the quantity of words addressed *directly to her* that is critical. '

hello & goodbye
from 18 months

This game helps develop your toddler's vocabulary and knowledge of routines and social conventions.

- When friends or relatives come to the door, encourage your toddler to greet them, or to say hello in response to their greetings. When they leave, show her how to wave or kiss them goodbye.

- Play a game where one of you goes outside and knocks on the door. The 'visitor' can pretend to be someone well known to the family or a complete stranger. The visitor and the person answering the door then introduce themselves and say hello. Invite the visitor in for a short activity that you and your child act out – this might be sharing a cup of tea, repairing something in the house or playing with toys together.

- Soon the visitor decides to leave, returns to the door and says 'Goodbye (see you again, see you later...).'

telephone talk
from 2 years

This make-believe game develops your child's language skills and concepts about time.

- Give your child a telephone of her own (a toy one, or a spare real one).

- Each day, make her telephone 'ring' and say 'Oh! Your telephone is ringing! It must be your friend _____.' Then talk to your child on your own telephone, in the same room but with a visual barrier between you.

- Disguise your voice and pretend to be the friend who is calling. Ask your child about her day, then finish by suggesting that you talk again tomorrow. The next day play the game again.

let's take turns
from 18 months

- **Snacks** Place a bowl of bite-sized pieces of fruit, cheese, cereal or biscuit between you and your child. Say 'One for you (giving your child a piece), and one for me?' (asking your child for one); 'Now, one for you,' and so on, until all the snacks are eaten.

- **Shopping** At the supermarket, point out different sections of the shop to your toddler, then take turns choosing which section to select groceries from next. Point out when it's 'my turn' or 'your turn'.

This activity reinforces ideas about taking turns and following rules when playing games.

fancy dress
from 2 years

Helping your child dress herself encourages self-confidence and a sense of achievement, but in this game language skills are also enhanced.

- Together, collect some interesting old clothes in a box or old suitcase and check that your child knows the name of each article.

- Ask her to close her eyes and choose an item. Keeping her eyes closed, see if she can guess what it is.

- If she guesses correctly, let her put it on. If she can't guess, let her choose another piece of clothing until she is successful.

- Now it is your turn to close your eyes and guess what item of clothing you have chosen. Your toddler lets you put it on if you guess correctly.

- Continue taking turns. You could both end up in some odd outfits – three hats, one shoe and so on.

cooking exploits

from 18 months

- Invite your child to help you bake a cake, biscuits, small pizzas, a pie, or even homemade modelling dough.

- Let her see you reading the recipe. Have her help to measure out and name the ingredients, pour them into the bowl or wash berries for a pie.

- Describe in detail to your child everything that happens.

- Give her a turn to whisk, mash and mix ingredients, crack eggs and sift flour.

- She can help sprinkle sugar on pie crusts, put raisin faces on biscuits or use her own selection of ingredients to build a mini pizza.

- Explain how long she will have to wait for the dish to cook in the oven, showing her how the clock will look when the time is up.

Young children love to be involved in a baking project. It will enhance language and fine motor skills as well.

RESEARCH SAYS

‘ Toddlers don't recognize that they are separate little people until the second half of their second year, when some may pass the 'mirror test'. First, a child looks in a mirror. Next, away from the mirror, a dab of paint is put on her face. Back in front of the mirror, she may recognize the change and try to wipe off the paint. ’

choices
from 18 months

- During everyday activities, offer your toddler choices as often as possible: 'Would you like to wear your white shirt or your blue shirt? Play outside or inside?'

- Your 2-year-old will enjoy this choosing game: fill a small bag with a favourite snack such as raisins or small biscuits and put two large mugs upside down between you. Tell your child you are going to hide a snack under one of the mugs, so she should close her eyes.

- Your child must then guess which mug is hiding the snack. If she is correct, reward her by giving her the snack. If not, repeat the game.

- Later on, switch roles. Your child hides the snack while you guess which mug it is under.

A child of this age enjoys making choices and it helps to build both her vocabulary and her ability to think logically.

bedtime
from 2 years

Toddlers absolutely love the bedtime routine. This game will enhance your child's concept formation and language abilities.

- At any time during the day, play the bedtime game. Choose a favourite stuffed toy, then together put the toy to bed.

- Make the bedtime routine as elaborate as you like and use a few props: a toy baby's bottle, towel, blanket, pillow, book and so on.

- Play other versions of this game where your toddler puts you to bed or you put her to bed.

looking after my friend

from 2 years

- Place items at separate 'daily routine stations' around a room, as follows: a favourite stuffed toy put 'to bed' with a blanket and pillow; some clothing for this toy; a breakfast snack in a bowl; a toothbrush; some toys to play with; a lunch snack on a plate; a washcloth; and finally, by the door, an outdoor object or toy (tricycle, ball, baby stroller).

- Now say 'Oh look, your friend (teddy) has come for a visit. Time to help him get up.' Show your toddler how to help teddy get up and make his bed.

- Follow with visits to get teddy dressed, eat breakfast, brush teeth, play with toys, eat lunch, wash hands and face, and finally, to the door to go out to play.

Daily routines make children feel secure. This game involves acting out some of these, building language and intellectual abilities.

RESEARCH SAYS

❛ There is no three-word stage in language development. Toddlers remain for several months in the two-word phase while their vocabularies build. Then, early in the third year, they begin to string four or more words together. ❜

AA in & out of the bath
from 18 months

Bathtimes provide an excellent opportunity for learning about opposites.

- Before your child gets into or out of the bath, ask her 'Is it time to climb *in* the bath or *out*?' Emphasize the words 'in' and 'out'.

- Once she is in, say 'You are *in* the bath.' Now point out other things that are also in the bath and have your child name them.

- Lift objects out of the water and explain 'Now the sponge (boat, soap, cup...) is *out* of the bath!' Ask your child to take other items out and name them – and those that remain in the bath.

- Use bathtimes to demonstrate other opposites such as big and small, cold and hot, wet and dry, shiny and dull.

RESEARCH SAYS

6 Parents direct more negative statements and prohibitions towards boys, and fathers issue more commands to sons. As a result, by age 4 as many as 36 per cent of boys' utterances to each other are either direct imperatives or prohibitions, versus 12 per cent for girls. 9

dinner delicacies

from 18 months

Games involving make believe boost your child's imagination and memory, plus her ability to use language.

● Prepare a pretend dinner in a sandbox. You will need plastic crockery and some utensils. Supply wet (water), dry (sand) and solid (small blocks) cooking ingredients.

● Ask your toddler what she would like to cook for dinner and then take turns 'cooking' parts of it. Your child might pour the 'peas' into the saucepan, you add water, she puts it on the 'stove' to cook, and so on.

● Each time one of you completes a step in the 'cooking' process, ask your child what needs to happen next.

what to wear?

from 2 years

This game is designed to accelerate verbal reasoning and logical thinking skills.

● On four cards, draw simple weather pictures: bright yellow sun; dark grey clouds and raindrops; a snowman and snowflake dots; a pale yellow sun and clouds.

● Prepare four piles of clothing to match these weather conditions: a bathing suit and sunglasses; an umbrella and boots; mittens, hat and scarf; a pullover.

● Show your child one of the pictures and ask her to choose the right pile of clothes for that kind of weather. Have her dress up in these items and, together, act out appropriate sunny, rainy, snowy or cloudy weather activities. Then show her another picture and continue the game in the same way.

fun at home

Easy activities and naming games around the house.

Everyday objects around the home can be used to great effect and toddlers love searching games. Naming games and stimulating activities such as treasure hunts will help to improve your child's speech and memory as well as their creative thinking. Remember to praise your child and spend time in one-on-one conversations about what you are doing around the house.

rainbow treasure hunt

from 18 months

Toddlers really enjoy searching games – this one helps to teach your child colour names as well as how to count.

- Say to your toddler 'Let's go on a treasure hunt! Shall we see how many colourful things we can find?' Give him a bag to collect things in.

- Ask him 'What colour should we look for first?' Then find small objects around the house of different colours in turn: a red apple, a green sock, an orange crayon and so on.

- Each time an object is found, compare its colour to a known object: 'This bright blue colour is the same as your T-shirt, isn't it?'

- At the end, together count how many different-coloured objects were found.

- Give your toddler some 'treasure', matching this to the number of colours found (six corn flakes, seven crayons, eight raspberries...).

RESEARCH SAYS

' Parents who consistently respond in positive, encouraging tones to their children's speech and behaviour tend to raise more verbally gifted children. '

soup pot

from 2 years

Playing this game is an excellent way to enhance your child's verbal memory.

- You will need a large saucepan with lid, a large wooden spoon and a basket of small objects. Say 'Let's make soup!' and have your child remove the lid of the pan.

- Ask 'What do you think we should have in our soup?' Let him choose an object from the basket, tell you what it is and place it in the saucepan.

- Then it's your turn. Say 'I think we should put some socks in the soup!' When there are three ingredients in the soup, ask your child to stir it and put on the lid.

- Scratch your head and ask 'Now, what is in our soup? Can you remember what delicious things are in it?' See if he can recall the ingredients.

find the room

from 2 years

A good way to enhance your child's visual-spatial memory and vocabulary, this game combines speech and movement.

- Walk around the house with your child, saying 'This room is the kitchen, now let's go and find the bathroom.' Locate the bathroom together and then ask 'Can you find the kitchen now?' See if your child can find it. Introduce other rooms in the same way.

- Then spin your child around three times and say 'Perhaps I can muddle your thinking! I expect you won't be able to find the sitting room now!' See if he can locate the correct room. Repeat this for other rooms.

- Later, instead of naming the room, describe it: 'Can you find the room where we cook our food?'

match me up
from 18 months

- Collect pictures of things your toddler can easily find in your house: fruit, toys, furniture or household objects.

- Show your child a picture. Say 'Oh look! Here is a picture of an apple. I know there is a real apple around here somewhere. Can you find it?'

- At first, make the game easier by ensuring that picture and object are in the same room.

- Have your child bring the object to you and compare it to the picture. Discuss together how the pictured and the real objects differ.

Speed up your child's vocabulary development with this pre-reading activity.

poor things!
from 2 years

This game has been designed to improve listening comprehension, and visual and verbal memory.

- While your child is not watching, select a number of familiar items from different rooms.

- Place your collection in front of her and say, 'Oh look! Poor things! This one is a pillow and this is a toothbrush (hold them up for display), but they are not happy! One belongs in the bedroom and one in the bathroom.'

- Ask 'Do you think you might be able to put them where they will be happy again?' Then see if your child can take the pillow to the bedroom and the toothbrush to the bathroom.

- Tell her how clever she is, then return to the pile of items and choose two more.

let me out!

from 2 years

- Collect a set of toys or picture cards to a category in which your child shows a special interest. Put them in a cardboard box and cut a hole in the lid large enough to put a hand through.

- Explain to your child that 'These dinosaurs (vehicles, dogs) want to come out, but they can't unless we can remember their names. Shall we try to help?'

- Take turns to pull out dinosaurs, name them, and describe where they are going. For example: 'Oh! This is diplodocus and he's plodding off to eat plants in this swamp over here.'

- Continue until there are no dinosaurs left in the box. If she has difficulty in remembering a name (make sure you have some difficulty from time to time), the dinosaur is returned to the box and the other player takes a turn.

Play this game when your child is showing an interest in a category of items or animals – such as dinosaurs, vehicles or dogs – to increase her vocabulary rapidly.

RESEARCH SAYS

❝ When your toddler can say 50–100 words she will be capable of grouping things in categories. ❞

finders, keepers?

from 18 months

- Give your toddler a shopping bag and say 'Let's go and find things!' Then lead her to a room that is not too cluttered with objects.

- Name a small object you think your child might recognize. For example: 'I see an alarm clock! Can you see an alarm clock? The alarm clock is ticking.' Use the name of the object as many times as you can and give hints if necessary to help her find the object.

- Continue to name more objects, extending the search to several rooms. After collecting three or four objects, each player takes a turn to pull one out of the bag and tries to remember where it was found, then returns it to its original location.

Especially appealing to toddlers, this game combines speech and movement. As a bonus, it increases visual memory.

colourful stranger

from 18 months

Teaching your toddler how to classify things according to shape and colour is an excellent way to develop her vocabulary and critical thinking.

- Choose three small toys or objects of the same colour and shape – for example, three red blocks. Show these to your child, explaining that they are all the same colour, and ask 'What colour are they?'

- Now cover the objects with a cloth and slip extra objects of the same type, size or shape but a different colour underneath – for example, a yellow block.

- Have your child remove the cloth, then say 'Oh dear, there's a strange one that doesn't belong with the others. Can you find the one that doesn't belong? The one that is not the same as all the rest?'

air brushing
from 2 years

- On large index cards, draw big shapes with coloured felt pens: a straight vertical line, straight horizontal line, circle, square and triangle.

- Turn your shape cards face down. Invite your child to choose a card and then name or describe the shape.

- Now have your child copy you as you slowly draw the shape in the air with your finger. Take turns practising.

- Then say 'Would you like to try that on paper?' Hold your child's finger gently and help her to draw the shape on a large sheet of paper using her finger.

- Continue with 'Well done! You did that so well! I bet you could draw (paint) a (name the shape) using your crayon (felt pen, paintbrush)!'

- Encourage your toddler to draw as slowly as possible, then as she improves see how quickly she can draw the shape.

This game is especially good for boys, whose fine motor skills tend to lag behind those of girls.

RESEARCH SAYS

❝ While word-learning circuits in the brain begin to mature at 2 years, those responsible for grammatically correct speech do not come into play until the age of 4. ❞

presents

from 18 months

Learning how to take turns and how to say 'please' and 'thank you' are easily taught in this game.

- Fill a container with small toys or household objects, and sit with your toddler. Say 'Would you like to play a game? This game is called Presents.'

- Explain: 'We need to take *turns*. First, it's your *turn* to have a present. Can you say "Please may I have a present?"' Encourage your toddler to say these words and immediately give him one of the items.

- Say 'Now it's my *turn* to have a present. Please may I have a present?' Have your child give you one of the items.

- Thank your child and name the item: 'Oh! Thank you. It's an eggcup!'

- Have your child copy this by saying 'thank you' and naming the item in his next turn. Emphasize the word 'turn' so that he begins to understand it.

- Continue playing until all the 'presents' are gone.

RESEARCH SAYS

❛ Language development is greatly accelerated when parents provide lots of positive feedback. Try to confirm, repeat and praise what your child says as much as possible. ❜

sound & seek
from 18 months

Toddlers enjoy imitating animal noises. This game teaches terms used to describe these noises and pairs them with the animals that make them.

- Tell your child you are a duck (or other animal) and you are going to hide. Explain: 'Listen for my quacks. When you hear me quacking, see if you can find me! Don't come until you hear my quacks.' When you have hidden, quack loudly and see if your toddler can find you.

- Then let him choose what animal he would like to be and what noise he will make as a signal for you to find him. Continue to take turns in this way.

- Your toddler will enjoy the game all the more if you have some difficulty finding him and behave as if you are slightly deaf!

alphabet pictures
from 18 months

Your child will love this picture identification game as it provides an opportunity to practise walking and running, as well as to learn new vocabulary.

- Mount an alphabet frieze on the wall at child height. Choose three of the items pictured that you think he might recognize – for example, an apple, a teddy and a cat. Discuss these pictures with your toddler, drawing attention to their colours and various parts.

- Now stand about 1.5m (5ft) away from the frieze with your child and say 'Look at all the pictures!' Ask 'Now where did that apple go? Can you find it?' See if your toddler can run and point to the correct picture. Then ask 'Are you clever enough to find another picture? Where did the picture of the teddy go? Can you find the teddy?'

- Soon your child will be able to find all three pictures easily and you can gradually introduce new ones.

AA shifty eyes

from 2 years

This game helps your child rapidly translate what his eyes see into sounds or words, and is good preparation for reading.

- Play this game when your child can name colours easily.

- Apply a piece of tape to a tabletop in a long horizontal line. Place two (or three, or four) different-coloured objects side by side on the line at the left-hand end.

- Now have your child 'read' the colours from left to right as fast as he can. For example: 'Green, blue, red!'

- As a reward, allow him to pick up the furthest left object and 'leap-frog' it over the other two, travelling to the right.

- Now encourage him to read this new configuration as fast as he can: 'Blue, red, green!'

- See if he can continue until the three objects reach the end of the line.

- As he improves, add more colours. You could also play this game using shapes or numbers written on cards.

RESEARCH SAYS

6 The age at which children begin talking varies widely and cannot be used to predict language skills at school age. 9

train game
from 18 months

Speed naming of objects, helps to reinforce neural pathways in many regions of a child's brain.

- Place three objects in a row in front of your child. Say 'Look, I've made a train: here's the front, the middle and the end.' Point to the objects from left to right.

- Ask 'What is this part of the train really? And this? And this?' Point to each object and have your toddler identify it. Then ask 'Can you do that faster now?' See if he can name the objects more quickly. Say 'That was excellent! Can you do that even faster now?'

- When he succeeds, exclaim 'Well done! Let's make the train longer.' Add another object to the right-hand end. Ask your child to name the new object and then all four objects as fast as he can, from left to right. Continue in this way and see how long you can make the train.

alphabet trip
from 2 years

Notice how your child's self-esteem and confidence builds as he progresses further with each journey.

- Once your child is adept at Alphabet Pictures (see page 51), stand in front of the frieze at Aa and ask 'Would you like to go on a trip? OK – this is where the journey starts.'

- Then explain that he should name each picture as it appears. He should see how fast he can go and how far he can 'travel' from left to right. When he can no longer name a picture or begins to tire, say 'Well done! You travelled a long way! You named six pictures! So come back 'home' now and I will welcome you with six kisses (treats, hugs). Clever boy!'

- Then play again and see how far he can now 'travel'.

naughty fruit

from 18 months

This vocabulary-building game uses a variety of fruits (or vegetables) and will appeal to your child's desire to handle different objects.

- Help your toddler understand that there are different kinds of fruit. Name and discuss as many of these as you can at home or in the supermarket.

- Place four or five different fruits in a bowl and say 'Look at all the fruit! This one is bright orange. Does it feel a bit bumpy? (let your child handle it) Do you know its name?'

- Discuss the other fruits in the same way. Then, when your toddler is not looking, scatter all the fruits over the table or floor.

- Exclaim 'Oh no! Look at all the NAUGHTY fruit! They hopped out and ran away! We need to call them by name so they come running back!'

- Ask 'Do you know the name of any of those naughty fruit? Yes? Well done! Let's call it by name!' Encourage your child to repeat the name of the fruit with you while he makes it 'scamper' smartly back into the bowl.

- Continue until all the fruit is back in the bowl.

RESEARCH SAYS

❛ Encouraging a child to speak himself in response to you enhances language development dramatically. Simple exposure to language on television or radio, or in overheard conversations, does not help a child learn a language. ❜

who's doing what?

from 2 years

This game utilizes picture books to build your child's ability to understand and use nouns and verbs.

- Collect some simple books that depict animals or people doing different things. Read a book together and talk about the pictures.

- Then say 'Let's find the picture of the pig again. What is he doing?' Repeat the verb (action word) as often as possible: 'Yes, you're right, he is *rolling*. Where is he *rolling*? Does he like *rolling* in the mud?' Continue in this way with other pictures.

- Find books that show more than one person or animal on a page and ask 'Which one is waving? Who is peeping out of the box? Where is the rabbit hiding? What is the dog eating?' These questions will encourage your child to use new nouns (naming words).

squiggles

from 2 years

When your child is accomplished at Alphabet Pictures (see page 51), begin to draw attention to the 'squiggles' in the corner of each picture.

- Stand in front of the first picture together and point to the letter a, saying 'See this funny little squiggle up here? This is an aaa.' Pronounce the sound, not the name. Then say 'What does it say? It tells you that the name of the picture starts with an aaa sound. Can you hear it? Aaa-apple.' Ask him again what it says.

- Now move about 1.5m (5ft) away with your child and say 'Now where did the aaa go? Can you find the funny little squiggle that says aaa?'

- Gradually introduce more letters, being very careful to name them only by their sounds and not by their names.

lost & found
from 2 years

- Find three objects whose names you believe your toddler does not know – for example: a ruler, a cushion and a sponge. Arrange the objects in a row. Talk about each one in turn, naming it several times.

- Say 'Uh-oh! The ruler's wandering off. He's going to get lost!' Carry the ruler off and place it in a bizarre location, but within sight and easy reach for your toddler. Repeat for the cushion and the sponge, placing them in different odd locations.

- Then say 'It's time to find those things now. Can you find the ruler?' Have your child find it and bring it back. Repeat for the other two objects. Now see if he can arrange them in a row in their original sequence.

This game is useful for teaching your toddler three new words at once.

short orders
from 2 years

The purpose of this game is to improve verbal comprehension and memory, but it will also boost your toddler's fine motor skills, co-ordination and balance.

- Write some single-task orders on small pieces of paper, such as: walk backwards, throw the yellow bean bag, climb up and down the stairs, thread two of those curtain rings on to this shoelace.

- Place all the order slips inside a clear jar with a lid. Shake the jar and ask your child to remove the lid and select an order.

- Read it to him and see how quickly he can follow the simple instruction.

- Then let him select another order.

strange menu

from 2 years

- Display 20 or 30 small objects in one corner of the room on a large cloth. Place two plastic bowls (or plates) here as well.

- Seat yourself at a low table and call out 'Waiter! I'm ready to order!' Pretend to be looking at a menu and say 'I would like the pencil, the keys and the soap, please.' Name two (three, four or five) objects that you know are in the 'kitchen' corner.

- Your 'waiter' then has to remember what you ordered, go to the 'kitchen' and find the items. Placing the items in the bowls, he returns carrying something in each hand.

- He places these on the table in front of you, and if he listened carefully you will receive the correct order. Thank him enthusiastically, saying that it looks delicious. If he brings the wrong items, re-order.

This is a game of make believe that has dramatic brain-building effects. If possible, visit a restaurant with your child first, or share a picture book on the topic.

RESEARCH SAYS

‘ **When parents talk to their children they activate the social, emotional and linguistic circuits of their child's brain all at once, but the influence on the developing language systems is the most profound.** ’

let's go

Words to discover when you're out and about.

When you are out of the house there is so much around that is exciting and novel for your child and he will be stimulated by new environments. He will love exploring, whether on a walk, at the shops or at the playground, and this will help improve his balance and co-ordination. The activities in this chapter will also encourage your child to use his observational skills and to relate to his new experiences.

twos

from 18 months

- Play this game when out for a walk or in the car.

- Name things as you pass by, saying 'Look! A tree!'

- Ask your toddler to look for another tree and point it out to you. Explain: 'Now we've found *two* trees. I saw a tree and you saw a tree. How many trees have we seen now?'

- Emphasize and repeat the word 'two', and encourage your child to use this word as well.

- Continue to point out and name things that you see, asking your toddler to find a second one.

Teach your child the names of things in his environment and how to count to two with understanding.

the boss

from 2 years

This game will accelerate your toddler's language abilities generally and enhance his verbal memory.

- Explain to your child that you are the 'boss' and he will only get paid if he can follow your orders. Have some 'money' in your pocket in the form of raisins or grapes, then proceed to give one-task orders: 'Run and touch that tree! Ride on the merry-go-round!'

- Each time your child follows the order, exclaim 'Well done!' and give him a piece of 'money'.

- When he can follow one-task orders without difficulty, give him orders with two steps: 'Throw the ball and pick it up again! Sit on the swing and stick out your tongue!' Eventually, your child may be able to follow a three-step order: 'Pick up the ball, bounce it on the ground and sit down!'

travel treasures
from 2 years

- Ask your toddler 'Would you like to travel in search of treasure?' Provide him with a box or backpack as a 'suitcase'.

- Say 'We begin the journey on a jet,' then with arms outstretched, zoom off to a random location in the park, garden or wherever you are.

- Invite your child to look for treasure here. Then say 'I can see a green pebble (red ball, orange leaf).' Have your toddler find this treasure and let him put it in his 'suitcase'.

- Explain 'Now we have to catch a train!' Then shuffle along together making choo-choo noises, until you reach a different 'country'.

- Continue travelling and hunting for treasure. Use different means of transport between locations.

A vocabulary-expanding game, this also provides your child with the opportunity to improve his balance and co-ordination.

RESEARCH SAYS

When a child hears and uses language it operates to shape the brain circuits that analyse speech sounds, interpret meaning and grammar, and control the ability to speak.

touching encounters

from 18 months

This vocabulary-building game can be played in the car, at the park or beach, out in the countryside, or anywhere there are unbreakable objects that your child can touch.

- If, for example, you are walking in the countryside, you might say 'That tree has interesting-looking bark. Let's see how it feels!'

- Then tell your toddler to close her eyes and feel the bark. Ask questions that give her a choice of answers: 'Does it feel rough or smooth?'

- Feel the bark yourself, saying 'Yes! You are right, it does feel smooth.'

- Then look for other things to touch, and talk about how they feel.

RESEARCH SAYS

❛ A child's language development is speeded up when parents' responses are attentive (the parent repeats, confirms or extends what the child says), warm (the parent gives more positive than negative feedback) and encouraging (the parent more often invites or asks than makes direct commands). ❜

shop talk
from 2 years

This is an easy way to enhance your child's observational and language skills, while you do the shopping!

- The supermarket is a great place to familiarize your toddler with different colours.

- Begin by pointing out the colour of something near you: 'Oh look, some yellow cheese! What else is yellow? Let's look for something else that is yellow.'

- If you see something yellow that your child has missed, point it out to her by asking 'Are those lemons yellow?'

- When you have found two yellow items, move on to a different colour. If your toddler points to an item she is not able to name, identify it for her.

- Then point out another colour and continue the game.

where did we go?
from 2 years

This game teaches vocabulary and concepts related to time. It will also help improve your child's memory and verbal skills.

- Help your child review the day's events by asking 'Where did we go today?' Help her recall what you did first, and discuss the details.

- Ask 'What did we do after that?' If she can't remember, prompt her. For example, say 'We were hungry, weren't we? Where did we go to have lunch?' Jog her memory to remember the details. Then ask 'After that, after lunch, what did we do?'

- When you have discussed all the things you did, review the day by listing in order four or five events. See how many of them your child can list in the correct order.

♫ round the mountain
from 18 months

You can play this vocabulary-boosting game at the beach, during a walk in the woods or in the countryside.

- Make up words to sing to the tune of *She'll Be Coming Round the Mountain*. For example: 'He'll be galloping (hopping, tip-toeing, zooming) round the mountain when he comes...'

- Sing the words as you and your child act them out.

- Then make the words more descriptive and as silly as possible: 'He'll be waddling like a duck (leaping like a frog, trotting like a horse) when he comes.'

- Later, make the movements even more complex by singing a second verse: 'He'll be patting at his head (blowing his trombone, quacking like a duck, looking right and left) as he gallops (hops, tip-toes, zooms).'

RESEARCH SAYS

❛ Language development is critically shaped by experience. The language networks of a child's brain wire up properly and permanently only when exposed to the sounds, meaning and grammar of a human language. ❜

slippery places
from 2 years

In this game, you increase your toddler's verbal abilities by asking silly questions about where you are going.

- When out in the town, ask questions like: 'Does the baker sell bread or fish? Will the dentist look at my knees or my teeth?'

- Later, make the game more challenging by deliberately making ridiculous remarks: 'We need to return to the parking meter to put in some more potatoes.'

- If at first your child does not notice your errors, repeat what you have said and seek agreement from him.

- When your child does notice, tell him how clever he is and how absolutely silly you are.

my favourite things
from 2 years

Amuse an older toddler during long journeys or waiting times with this speech sound game.

- Tell your child your name is Sss-simon (Sss-sally), drawing out the beginning sound, and you only like things that sound the same as the beginning of your name – 'things that begin with sss!' Ask 'Can you think of something I would like?'

- Your child asks you 'Would you like (biscuits, ham)?' Each time you shake your head and say 'no'. As soon as he says a word that starts with the sss sound (slugs, sausages...), you say 'Yes! I love sss-slugs!'

- Continue until he has thought of three words that begin with the sss sound and then become a different character, changing your name. Names that start with S, M, F, N, V are best to begin with, as the beginning sounds can be drawn out and emphasized more easily than other letter sounds.

pet detective

from 18 months

- When your toddler is not looking, hide various animal toys around the garden and then say 'I can't find your teddy bear, or your sheep, or your giraffe. I think they must have come outside to play, too.'

- Say 'Maybe they are lost. Shall we look for them?' Stroll around, then say 'Oh! I can see something brown behind that tree. Who is it?'

- See if your child can name the animal as she retrieves it.

- Continue the search for the remaining animals, each time giving your toddler clues about their location.

Playing this hide-and-seek game teaches descriptive vocabulary.

clueless

from 2 years

This game boosts verbal reasoning skills and language development while keeping your child amused during a long wait or car journey.

- Tell your child that your name is Clueless. Your brain doesn't work properly. You can think about things but you can't remember their names. Ask 'Would you like to help me think of the names of things?'

- If you have a son, he will be interested in the properties of objects. Ask him questions like: 'I'm thinking of something that ticks and tells the time (a machine that cleans carpet) – what is it called?'

- If you have a daughter, other people's behaviour will hold more fascination for her. Ask these kind of questions: 'I can't think of the name of the hair on grandpa's chin (what your grandmother wears to help her see better) – what is it called?'

silly milly

from 2 years

- Ask your toddler if she would like to play Silly Milly (Silly Billy).

- Explain 'I will tell you something silly to do, and then you think of something silly for me to do. Are you ready?'

- Then say 'Make your ears wave at me!', or 'Flap your arms like wings!', or 'Purr like a cat!'

- Your toddler follows this command, then it's her turn to give you a silly command.

- If she is unable to think of something that does not require you to move too far from the spot, take another turn yourself until something occurs to her.

This vocabulary-building and creativity-boosting game is ideal for those testing times when you are waiting in a queue.

RESEARCH SAYS

'Parents can help their child's language development by using a variety of words and sentence structures, and by making connections between an unknown word and words she already knows.'

postman
from 18 months

Some preliminary preparation is required for this symbol-matching and naming game.

- You will need to establish several 'residences' around the garden (start with three). Using stiff index cards, draw a symbol on each. Begin with simple shapes: circle, square, triangle, rectangle. Attach the cards at various sites at your child's height. These are the 'addresses' of the dwellings.

- Using either real envelopes or index cards, make a set of 'letters'. Address each, in this case, with a shape.

- Give your toddler a bag containing the letters and examine them together, discussing their addresses. Then see if she can deliver the letters to the correct houses by matching the addresses.

- When your toddler knows the names of the shape symbols, vary the game by addressing the letters and labelling the houses with numbers or letters.

RESEARCH SAYS

'Babies as young as 13–15 months actually notice the grammar and word order in sentences, and use this information to help them understand what is being said.'

nature match

from 18 months

This is an excellent language game to play when you and your toddler are out for a walk.

- Draw your child's attention to an eyecatching leaf (flower, shell, pebble, seed pod...). Talk about its shape, colour and size, then say 'I wonder if we can find another one the same?'

- Help your child find a matching object, then explain that now you have 'two the same' you have a matching 'pair'.

- Then find another object and try to create another matching pair. See how many matching pairs you can find during your walk.

bus, car, jeep, van

from 2 years

This spot-the-object and counting game can be played when you are out walking or in the car.

- Challenge your child to spot different kinds of vehicles. Say 'Let's take turns and see how many different kinds of machines are on the road today!'

- Have your child count on her fingers as different vehicles are spotted: 'Car! That's one!' Show her how to hold on to one finger.

- Next, she may point to and name a bus. Show her how to hold on to two fingers. If your child points to a vehicle she cannot name, tell her what it is and show her how to hold on to another finger.

- Aim to find five different kinds of vehicles, one for each finger of one hand. Gradually increase the target number and have her count fingers on both hands.

slides & swings

from 2 years

- Give a description of one piece of equipment: 'It's something silver that has a ladder and a chute you can slide down; it's something to sit on that swings back and forth.' See if your child can locate it quickly, run over to it and tell you its name.

- If she succeeds, praise her and tell her that as a reward, she may play on the slide (swing, rope ladder...) for two minutes. Time this, then give her another description.

- Each time your child locates and names the equipment correctly, let her play on it for a minute or two as a reward. If she has difficulty, describe another piece of equipment and see if she can locate and name that one.

Help your child learn the names of the equipment in a playground by repeating them often, as she plays on each one. Then play this game.

jungle safari

from 2 years

Play this game outside in a place where there are some trees and low shrubs. It will teach your child verbal comprehension, verbal memory and listening skills.

- Tell your child that you will count to 20 and as soon as you reach 20 she should stop moving. During this time she must find a place to hide.

- Tell her: 'I'm going to stay here and pretend to be a big lion. When I stop counting it means I am asleep.' Continue with: 'Try to sneak up for a closer look at me. But watch out! If I hear any noise I will wake up and try to see you!'

- Count to 20, close your eyes and listen for noises. See how close your child can get to you without being seen. Take turns to be the lion and the person on safari.

obstacle race

from 2 years

- Set up an obstacle course for your toddler: a 'valley' (cardboard box) to climb in and out of, a 'huge mountain' (upturned laundry basket) to circumnavigate, a large 'lake' (green or blue tablecloth or blanket) to swim across, some 'stepping stones' (cushions or paper plates) to negotiate, and so on.

- At first, keep the obstacles to a minimum. As your child improves, gradually increase the number.

- Show her the target destination, where the enticing prize or refreshment awaits. Show her where to start the 'race' and announce 'Ready! Set! Go!'

- Help her negotiate the course, and as she progresses talk about each obstacle, naming it repeatedly.

- Later, vary the game by timing the race and challenge her to name each obstacle before negotiating it.

This game boosts many varied skills including visual and verbal memory, vocabulary, co-ordination, balance and creativity.

RESEARCH SAYS

❛ Children spoken to most by their parents during the first 3 years of life end up with superior reading, spelling, speaking and listening abilities 5 years later. ❜

what's that sound?

Helping your toddler recognize familiar noises.

Toddlers love making noise, and by encouraging them to repeat familiar household sounds and animal noises you can help them to learn about tone and pitch. The fun activities in this chapter will help them to concentrate on important listening skills such as discriminating where a sound is coming from and whether it is loud or soft. Singing is also a great way to make every-day activities more enjoyable and memorable.

high & low
from 18 months

- Walk around the house together and point to various objects, asking 'What's that?' Encourage your toddler to identify the object by name.

- Then ask 'Can you tell me what this is called in a tiny, little, high voice like this?' Demonstrate how to say the word in a high voice and encourage her to copy you.

- Point to another object for your toddler to name and then ask 'Can you tell me its name in a big, deep, low voice like this?' Demonstrate how to say the word in a very low voice and encourage her to copy you.

- Continue in this way, having your child name things in either a high or a low voice.

This game trains your toddler's ability to hear high- and low-pitched voices.

bus trip
from 2 years

Singing songs together will help your child to concentrate on the sounds heard in speech, which is important when learning to read and spell.

- Teach your child *The Wheels on The Bus* song: 'The wheels on the bus go round and round (repeat 'round and round' three times), The wheels on the bus go round and round all through the town.'

- Then: the horn on the bus goes beep, beep, beep; the doors... go open and shut; the wipers... go swish, swish, swish; the people... go up and down; the baby... goes 'Waah, waah, waaa'; the bell... goes ding, ding, ding. Sing this song and act out the words together.

- Adapt the words to other forms of transport: the wheels on the train go clickety-clack....

♫ I'm a little teapot

from 2 years

- Teach your toddler the song and actions for *I'm a Little Teapot*: 'I'm a little teapot short and stout, Here's my handle and here's my spout, When I get all steamed up then I shout, Tip me over and pour me out.'

- When your child knows this song well, talk about the sounds made by other objects around the house. Using the same tune, change the words and actions to suit the object. For example: 'I'm a little telephone quiet for a while, Here's my handle and here's my dial, When someone telephones then I sing, Pick me up and stop the ring.'

- Discuss the sounds made by a clock, kitchen kettle, sprinkler or jack-in-the-box toy, and make up words and actions for these objects.

This singing activity helps to develop vocabulary and listening skills.

RESEARCH SAYS

6 **One auditory ability that is rather poor in young children is sound discrimination in a noisy setting. When they are learning the subtleties of speech, it is best if background noise can be kept to a minimum.** **9**

who's talking?

from 18 months

Children are fascinated by animal noises. This game helps your child learn the vocabulary used to describe these sounds.

- Show your child two stuffed toy animals – for example, a dog and a sheep – and make each animal 'talk'.

- Say 'Oh! Listen! Here's the dog! The dog is saying woof, woof, woof! And here is the sheep. The sheep says baa, baa, baa.'

- Ask your toddler to close her eyes and listen. Then make one of the animal noises and ask 'Who is talking? Is it the dog or the sheep?'

- Help your child to guess which one, or demonstrate again what each animal 'says'.

- Gradually introduce more animals and animal noises for your toddler to identify.

RESEARCH SAYS

'From 3 to 6 months, a baby's ability to hear high-pitched sounds begins to develop; by 7 years, children can hear the highest tones better than adults. The ability to hear low-pitched sounds, however, matures much more slowly, improving very gradually until a child reaches puberty.'

soft & loud
from 2 years

This game involves trying to imitate the sounds heard in the environment, an activity that demands close attention.

- Listen for sounds together at home, in the car, or while out and about. Try to imitate the noises heard, asking your child 'Can you make that noise?'

- Then say 'I can't hear you. I'm a bit deaf. Can you make the sound very loudly, please?' Encourage your child to make the noise loudly.

- Then say 'Oh! I have very sensitive ears! Can you make that sound very quietly, please?' Then see if your child can make the sound very quietly.

- Ask her to say things to you in a big, loud voice and in a tiny, quiet voice, and teach her how to have conversations where you both whisper.

what makes this noise?
from 2 years

Once your child is used to playing Soft & Loud (see above) and can identify sounds in the environment, try making up your own for her to listen to.

- Make some sounds and see if your child can identify what would make them.

- If you give her a choice of answers, she will find this a lot easier.

- You might say 'Hoo, hoo: is that the wind blowing or the thunder booming?' or 'Tick, tick, tick: is that water dripping or a clock ticking?' or 'Ding-dong, Ding-dong: is that the noise of jingle bells or a door bell?'

AA sound detectives
from 18 months

Enhance your toddler's ability to concentrate and distinguish particular sounds from everyday background noise.

- Sit down with your toddler and ask 'Can you hear any noises in this room?'

- Help him locate the source of any sounds he hears and identify what made them. Then say 'Listen carefully. Can you hear any sounds coming from the next room (kitchen, bathroom, outdoors...)?'

- Each time, go and locate the source of the noise and identify what made it.

- Then, in this new location, listen together for more sounds to identify.

- Each time you play, begin the game in a different room.

RESEARCH SAYS

' Babies grow steadily quicker and more precise at locating sounds during their first 6 months. This ability then continues to improve very gradually, until a child is about 7 years old. '

weather sounds

from 2 years

While enhancing language development, this game also helps to improve your child's ability to concentrate and listen carefully.

- When out for a walk or in the car, ask your child 'What kind of day is it today? How does it sound?'

- Ask other questions to draw his attention to the sounds that accompany different conditions: 'Can you hear the raindrops pitter-pattering on the roof? Why are the buses and trees making so much noise today?'

- Talk about the sounds made by feet crunching on frost, swishing through leaves or squelching in wet mud. Discuss how wet days sound different to dry ones – car tyres on wet roads or puddles splashing.

- Tell your child to close his eyes and see if he can guess what kind of day it is, just by listening.

surrounding sounds

from 2 years

Develop your child's ability to identify where sounds are coming from.

- Go for a walk with your child and find a place to sit down together. Then say 'Let's see what sounds we can hear.' Have your child close his eyes to improve his concentration. Ask 'Can you hear a sound yet?'

- When he hears a specific sound, tell him to keep his eyes closed and point to where it was coming from.

- With eyes open, together follow the direction in which he is pointing and see how accurate his ears were. Say 'Let's follow the direction and get closer. Is this the right direction? Shall we get even closer?' Take turns to listen and point. Sometimes the direction might be straight up, in which case simply look up.

AA fast talk, slow talk

from 18 months

Combining speech and movement is one of the best ways to boost language and listening skills.

- Demonstrate various movements – marching, jumping, running, spinning, bending, waving, wiggling – and teach your child the name of each one.

- As you march around the room or outdoors, say 'Let's march! March, march, march...' Encourage your toddler to copy you while saying the word 'march' in time to her movements.

- After a short time, suggest another movement: 'Let's sway! Sway, sway, sway...' Again, have your child copy your movements and join you in saying the word 'sway'.

- At first, say the words and move in time to them very slowly. Later, alternate 'fast talk' with 'slow talk', so that sometimes you and your toddler talk and move very slowly and sometimes very quickly.

RESEARCH SAYS

6 Children who have difficulty discriminating sounds that change within fractions of a second are likely to have problems using and understanding speech. This ability improves in children between the ages of 3 years and puberty. 9

transporting sounds

from 2 years

This game teaches vocabulary associated with vehicle noises and helps boost listening skills.

- Display pictures of various vehicles and/or toy vehicles, in a row so that your toddler can see them easily. Talk about the noise each vehicle makes and have your child copy the noises.

- Then say 'Now are you ready to play a special game? Listen very carefully. Your ears must be very clever.' Explain: 'I am going to make a noise. See if you can find the picture or the toy that goes with that sound.'

- Make various vehicle sounds, helping your child to find a picture or toy vehicle that makes that sound.

- Start with three or four pictures or toys and gradually increase the number.

find the noisy one

from 2 years

Your child will enjoy this auditory and visual memory game.

- Collect some household objects or toys that make a noise, such as a bell, a rattle, or toy animals.

- Show the objects to your child, letting her make noises with each one. Discuss the noises as she does this. Then ask her to close her eyes while you use one of the objects to make a noise.

- After you have made the sound, tell your child to open her eyes and guess which object made the noise. Ask 'Which was the noisy one?'

- Take turns being the listener and the sound-maker.

who am I?

from 2 years

- Crawl around quickly, barking like a dog, and ask 'Who am I? Am I a dog or a rabbit?' Wiggle along on the floor saying 'Sss, sss, sss' and ask 'Who am I? Am I a lion or a snake?'

- Act out other animals, and gradually make your questions more difficult: 'Am I a snake or a lizard?' When your child is expert at this, take turns to act out animals for the other player to guess.

In this auditory and visual memory game you pretend to be an animal and ask your child to guess who you are.

farm animals

from 2 years

An excellent all-round brain-booster, in this game your child listens for the sounds of farmyard animals and has to identify them.

- Look at picture books about farm animals with your child and make all the animal noises together. Or, teach your child to sing *Old Macdonald Had a Farm*.

- Ask him if he would like to be the farmer. Then tell him to stay in the corner of the 'field' (this can be indoors) until he hears one of the hungry farm animals calling.

- Now scamper off somewhere and hide. Pretend to be a cow (pig, horse, duck...) and call out loudly and repeatedly with the appropriate animal noise.

- Your child, the 'farmer', then comes to tend you. She will need to identify what animal you are in order to feed you your favourite food.

- Later, take turns to hide.

AA fine tuning

from 2 years

- Show your child two different toy vehicles that have different-sounding wheels, or two different whistles, or rattles. Demonstrate how each makes a different sound.

- Now say 'I bet I can guess which one is making a noise without looking.' Put your hands over your eyes.

- Instruct your child to make a noise with one of the objects. You might say 'Oh dear! I can't guess which one that is. Can you make its noise again?' Identify the object by describing its details: 'It's the blue plastic whistle' (not the paper whistle that rolls out).

- Let your child take a turn hiding his eyes and guessing which object you make a noise with. Later, increase the number of objects to three.

This is a more challenging listening game, which requires your child to discriminate between two similar sounds.

RESEARCH SAYS

❛ **Be particularly vigilant for symptoms of ear infections in your young child, since even very subtle changes in his early auditory experience can affect language development.** ❜

first songs
and rhymes

Enjoying simple tunes and finger games.

It is so rewarding to capture your toddler's attention by singing, and familiar tunes will make your child feel more secure and comfortable. The ideas given here feature nursery rhymes, tongue twisters and simple finger games to encourage number and language skills. Children love to know what comes next, and by repeating the same tunes again and again they will learn how to follow a sequence of actions.

AA flying by

from 18 months

You can expand this finger game into more verses by introducing different insects – but always keep the final verse the same.

- 'Here's a honey-bee, He sits on your arm, He walks a little, But he means no harm.' (Fingers land on your toddler's arm, then 'walk' up and down a little very gently.)

- 'Now here's a fly, He lands in your hair, He buzzes about, But you don't care!' (Fingers land softly on your child's hair and move about a little, making bzzz, bzzz noises.)

- 'Here's a mosquito, He thinks YOU taste right, Watch out for him! He wants a BITE! (Fingers zoom in, as you make high-pitched eee! eee! noises, and try to land on parts of your child's body; your other hand helps your child to bat the 'mosquito' away.)

RESEARCH SAYS

‘ Early childhood musical (or rhythm and rhyme) experiences, especially if they involve the parents, are one of the most powerful ways to accelerate the "wiring up" of a child's brain. ’

ten little bunnies

from 18 months

This is a good finger-play game for enhancing your toddler's number and vocabulary skills.

- 'Ten little bunnies hop out one day' (All ten fingers 'hop'.)

- 'To dig some holes' (All ten fingers 'dig' holes.)

- 'And to play and play' (All ten fingers scamper around.)

- 'Five have a nibble' (Fingers of one hand 'nibble'.)

- 'Five fall asleep' (The other fingers lie flat and still.)

- 'Then along comes a fox' (Your face looms in closer.)

- 'And... watch them LEAP!' (All fingers on each hand 'leap' off in opposite directions.)

four birdies & a cat

from 18 months

This finger-play will help to develop your toddler's counting skills.

- 'One little birdie twittering at you' (wiggle one finger.) 'Another one says "How do you do?"' (Hold up a finger on the other hand and make it 'talk' to the first finger.)

- 'Two little birdies twittering at you' (Hold up two fingers on the first hand, wiggling them a little.) 'Another one says "Let's coo and coo!"' (Hold up one finger on the other hand and make it 'talk' to the first two fingers.)

- Repeat the words and actions for the third finger, using the reply 'Another one says "Can I do it too?"' Holding up the fourth finger, reply 'Along comes a cat and he says... "Boo!"' (Hold up your thumb and make it 'pounce' on the other fingers, which all disappear quickly.)

♫ nursery rhymes

from 18 months

- Teach your toddler some simple nursery rhymes. Buy books, tapes and CDs that you can enjoy together, reciting and acting out the rhymes. Now change the words to make them more personal to your child. Try to include her name whenever possible.

- For example: 'Pat-a-cake, pat-a-cake, baker's man, Bake me a cake as fast as you can, Pat it and prick it and mark it with a T (C, B, D, G, P, V – if your child's name begins with one of these letters), And put it in the oven for (your child's name) and me.'

- Or, 'Hickory, dickory dock! (your child's name) ran up the clock, The clock struck one and _____ ran down, Hickory, dickory dock!'

Including your child's name in the words of familiar nursery rhymes will delight her.

AA to & fro in the snow

from 18 months

Your toddler will have fun reciting and acting out this rhyme in winter.

- If it is snowing outside or you have been reading a book about snow, recite this action rhyme together:

- 'Snow, snow, falls without a sound.' (Hold your arms up then lower them while making your fingers 'dance'.)

- 'Let's make an angel. Lie on the ground.' (Lie on the floor and move your arms up and down to make 'wings' in the 'snow'.)

- 'Snow, snow, look how softly it falls.' (As first action.)

- 'Uh-oh! Watch out for my snowballs!' (Pretend to 'throw' your snowballs.)

fun in the sun

from 18 months

- Draw your child's attention to the sunny day outside, then recite this rhyme in a slow, steady rhythm:

- 'Sun, sun, shining so bright' (Hold your arms over your head and bring them slowly down to form a big circle.)

- 'Let's swim, swim, out of sight' (Pretend to swim.)

- 'Sun, sun, shining so light' (Repeat first action.)

- 'Makes a swim feel just right!' (Pretend to swim.)

- Encourage your toddler to join in with your words and actions.

This rhyme will help your toddler develop concepts about weather conditions.

RESEARCH SAYS

❝ **Music stimulates all the senses, training your child's brain to organize and conduct numerous activities all at the same time.** ❞

cakes
from 18 months

Encouraging your toddler to copy these words and relatively complex actions will help improve his verbal memory, comprehension and fine motor skills.

- 'A little cake' (Make a fist.)

- 'A larger cake' (Cover your fist with your other hand.)

- 'A great big cake I see!' (Open out your hands, fingertips touching to make an even bigger ball shape.)

- 'Now let's count the cakes we made, One! Two! Three!' (Repeat the actions in sequence.)

- Change the words and actions for a 'hedgehog' (bear, lion) verse, starting as curled-up balls on the floor and making your bodies grow progressively bigger.

RESEARCH SAYS

‘Being exposed to speech is the most important form of stimulation a child's developing brain receives.’

this is the way

from 18 months

This is a traditional rhyme with a surprise ending that children love. Your toddler will pay very close attention to the words as a way of preparing himself.

- Place your child on your knees facing you and hold his hands. Then recite the rhyme:

- 'This is the way the gentleman rides – trit-trot, trit-trot, trit-trot.' (Alternate knees rise and fall at a sedate pace.)

- 'This is the way the lady rides – can-ter, can-ter, can-ter.' (Knees rock at a slightly faster pace.)

- 'This is the way the old man rides – hide-ee-hee, hide-ee-hee, hide-ee-hee. And – down into the ditch!' (Knee movements are jerky and slow, then tip your child gently off your knees.)

one to five

from 18 months

Performing this finger-play is an excellent way to introduce your toddler to early counting skills.

- Hold up your thumb: 'One, one, one, that's a thumb.'

- Hold up two fingers and say 'Two, two, two, eyes of blue.' (Gently touch each eye with each finger.)

- Three fingers: 'Three, three, three – all having tea.' (Draw the tips of the three fingers together.)

- Four fingers: 'Four, four, four – look at them roar!' (Flash the fingers up and down.)

- Now, hold up all five fingers, spread out, and say 'Five, five, five – let's take a dive!' (Align the fingers side by side and, like a diver, take your hand up, bend the fingers and swoop down into a steep 'dive'.)

♫ simple songs
from 18 months

- Songs where the words can be easily accompanied by actions are fun. When your toddler knows some, use familiar tunes to introduce new words.

- For example, describe what you or your toddler are doing by singing new words to the tune of *Row, Row, Row Your Boat*: 'Ride, ride, ride in the car (on the bus, on your 'trike', in the stroller, on mummy's knee, on daddy's shoulders...), Gently down the street, Merrily, merrily, merrily, merrily, I wonder who we'll meet?'

- The meaning might often end up a little ridiculous: 'Hide, hide, hide (wash, munch, play, sing, clap...) in the bin (sink, tree, bush, tub, box...), Gently for awhile, Merrily, merrily, merrily, merrily, This is just my style!'

Learning the words to simple songs is an excellent way to develop your child's language abilities.

♫ singing toys
from 18 months

This singing game will expand your toddler's knowledge and understanding of action words.

- Arrange animal toys or puppets around the room. Then sing this song to the tune of *Rock-A-Bye Baby*. 'My name is (Teddy), I like to play, Tell me your name, Please tell me, okay?' Have teddy approach another toy and pretend to be singing to it.

- The toy that was approached sings in return: 'My name is (Bunny), I like to play, "Bunny" is my name, But I'm (hopping) today.'

- Bunny hops off to the next animal and repeats the first words that teddy sang. Continue like this, moving each animal in a different way.

♫ fast planes & slow trains

from 18 months

- Sing this song to the tune of *Row, Row, Row Your Boat* and perform the actions:

- 'Fly, fly, fly your plane, Wherever you want to go, Merrily, merrily, merrily, We can go fast and slow.'

- Sing the song very slowly once or twice while you both fly (arms outstretched) around the room slowly. Then sing the song faster several times, zooming around much more quickly.

- Further verses could include: 'Drive, drive, drive your car; Paddle, paddle, paddle the canoe; Ride, ride, ride your horse', and so on. You can make this game all the more interesting for your toddler by supplying props, such as an improvised steering wheel.

Repetitive action songs are an excellent way to develop language, balance and timing.

RESEARCH SAYS

' After participating in a programme involving music, movement and drama, disadvantaged children's self-esteem scores were significantly higher. '

♫ let's bop

from 18 months

Many pop songs have catchy tunes and simple, repetitious words and rhythms that will boost your toddler's memory and enhance her awareness of rhythm and rhyme.

- Play some pop music for your toddler. Pick her up and dance together, or allow her to dance on your feet.

- Sing along to any songs you know and praise her when she joins in.

- Later, sing one of the songs unaccompanied and encourage her to join in.

- Give her a simple instrument such as a mouth organ or rattle and see if she can play it in time to the music.

- Take turns playing different instruments to various songs, encouraging your toddler to hum or sing along.

RESEARCH SAYS

6 Between 2 and 3 years, learning to hear the beat or rhythm in a song helps develop abilities that underlie learning to read and spell. However, parents may not be making the most of this time: studies show that only 10 per cent of kindergarten children are able to keep a steady beat. 9

one little chicken

from 18 months

Teaching your toddler the words and actions to this finger-play will have dramatic effects on her language, memory and fine motor skills.

- 'One little chicken, pecking at a crumb' (One finger 'pecks' at the table.) 'Another one says "Can I have some?"' (One finger on the other hand 'talks' to the first one.)

- 'Two little chickens pecking at a crumb' (Two fingers 'peck'.) 'Another one says "I'm your chum!"' (One finger on the other hand 'talks' to the first two fingers.)

- Repeat for the third finger, using the reply 'Another one says "I need to fill MY tummy-tum-tum!"'

- 'Four little chickens pecking at a crumb' (Four fingers 'peck' at the table.) 'Along comes a fox and he says – 'YUM!"' (The other hand 'bites' at the 'chickens'.)

follow the leader

from 2 years

This language- and memory-boosting game also promotes co-ordination and balance.

- Ask your child to stand behind you and try to copy what you do. Then start tip-toeing (marching, sliding...) or walk while arm-waving or clapping.

- Sing to the tune of *Twinkle, Twinkle, Little Star*: 'Twinkle, twinkle, do you see? Can you, can you, copy me?' Sing this several times, checking that she is copying you.

- Now ask your toddler to be the leader. Have her repeat the movements and sing a second verse several times: 'Twinkle, twinkle, I could see, Clever, clever, clever me!' Now you follow, copying her movements. Then you become the leader, sing the first verse again and invent a new way of moving for your toddler to copy.

rain refrain

from 18 months

This is a good action rhyme to perform together when it is too wet to play outdoors.

- Draw your toddler's attention to the rain outside.

- Recite the following rhyme in a slow, steady rhythm while performing the actions:

- 'The rain, the rain is pouring down.' (Reach each arm alternately up and down in front of you.)

- 'Puddles to jump in – but don't drown!' (Pretend to jump and fall in puddles.)

- 'The rain, the rain, is soaking our hair.' (Repeat the first action, but also pretend the rain is pouring down over your face.)

- 'But puddles are fun so we don't care!' (Continue to jump in 'puddles'.)

- Encourage your child to copy your actions, and if you repeat the rhyme over and over he will soon learn the words, too.

RESEARCH SAYS

'Preschool children who received training involving musical games and songs gained an IQ advantage of 10–20 points. Ten years later, they had higher reading and maths scores.'

rhymes on purpose

from 18 months

Playing with the sounds of language appeals to a child's sense of humour, and this activity speeds learning of the logic of grammar.

- Teach your toddler the well-known rhyme 'To market to market, to buy a fat pig, home again, home again, jiggety-jig.'

- Then, whenever you are on an outing you can adapt it to tell your toddler what is happening. Encourage him to recite with you and maintain the rhyming part.

- 'To market, to market, to buy some dinner (bread, eggs, bananas), Home again, home again, jiggety-jinner (jed, jegs, jananas).'

- 'To the checkout, the checkout, to pay some money, Home again, home again, jiggety-junny.'

rainbow song

from 2 years

This song will develop your child's memory, vocabulary and overall intelligence.

- First, teach your child to sing the well-known song *Baa, Baa, Black Sheep*.

- When he is familiar with the tune, teach him to sing these words to it: 'Red, orange, yellow, green, Blue and in-di-go, Vio–let! vio–let!, Don't forget!'

- Whenever you spot a rainbow in the sky, discuss the colours with your child and sing the song together.

- Paint rainbows together, discussing how to make the colours, or see if your toddler can arrange different-coloured crayons in the correct rainbow order.

tongue twisters
from 2 years

- Following the same pattern as *Fuzzy-Wuzzy was a Bear*, make up new rhymes:

- 'Slippy-Slimy was a snake, But Slippy-Slimy had no lake, So Slippy-Slimy wasn't slippy, slimy – was she?'

- 'Canny-Danny is a train, But Canny-Danny has no brain, So Canny-Danny cannot be canny Danny – can he?'

- Based on *How Much Wood Could a Woodchuck Chuck*:

- 'How many crocs would a crocodile dial, If a crocodile could dial crocs?'

Young children love to play with the sounds of language and these tongue twisters provide an early challenge.

letter-sound songs
from 2 years

When you have played Squiggles (see page 55) and your child can pronounce the *sound* of a letter in reponse to seeing its shape, play this game.

- Point to one of the lower-case letters on an alphabet frieze or in a book that your toddler can recognize and encourage her to join in as you sing to the tune of *Mary Had a Little Lamb*:

- 'This is the squiggle that says a-a-a, a-a-a, a-a-a, This is the squiggle that says a-a-a, A-a, a, A, a-a. Sing the letter *sound*, not the letter name. Repeat for other letters your child can recognize.

- Your child may begin to recognize lower-case letter shapes on signs, cereal boxes or in magazines. Join in with him as he sings the appropriate letter-sound song.

♫ find the letter

from 2 years

- Sing this song whenever there is an opportunity to draw your toddler's attention to a letter shape and sound with which he is familiar. Focusing on lower-case (rather than upper-case) letter shapes is far more useful for learning to read.

- Sing to the tune of *Mary Had a Little Lamb*: 'I can see a mm – mm – mm, a mm – mm – mm, a mm – mm – mm, It's somewhere on this page (box, wall, floor, door).'

- Then sing: 'Can you find the mm – mm – mm...? It's somewhere on this page.'

- See if your child can find the letter. Remember to use only letter *sounds* – knowing letter *names* causes some children substantial confusion later when learning to read.

This is an excellent game to teach your child the shapes of letters and their sounds – the most important factor in predicting reading ability.

RESEARCH SAYS

" A group of 3-year-olds were given 50 minutes a day of singing lessons while another group received piano lessons. After nine months, both groups showed amazing improvement in their ability to put together a puzzle, a way of measuring mathematical reasoning skill. "

making music

Musical fun using everyday household objects.

Most children are naturally drawn to music, and will gain a great sense of achievement by making up a tune or keeping a beat. The activities in this chapter encourage creativity and rhythm, and include making home-made instruments out of everyday objects like saucepans or cardboard tubes. The games also teach your child to memorize a sequence of words or actions, which will help their physical skills and language development.

jingle bells
from 2 years

- Gather some metal bracelets, keys, coins and blunt metal bolts. You will also need two clear jars with lids and some string.

- Help your child thread the string through the bracelets and tie them loosely together, then let him shake them.

- Ask him to fill a jar with the coins and close the lid. Now let him shake the jar and listen to the sound it makes.

- Help him to make more instruments by stringing the keys together and filling the jar with metal bolts.

- Let your child jingle one of his instruments in time to music. See if he can play and dance at the same time.

Making simple musical instruments to play can provide your child with hours of enjoyment. Only play this game if he has stopped putting things in his mouth.

pat-a-cake tambourine
from 2 years

Your child's self-esteem is enhanced when he makes his own musical toy to play in time to music.

- Help your child make a tambourine from two paper plates, string, and about ten jingly items.

- Punch four or five 1cm (¼in) holes evenly around the rim of each plate. Put the plates together to create a space inside, matching up the holes. Thread string through each pair of holes, tying loosely.

- Let him select two jingly items, then tie them together using the string at each pair of holes. Show him how to hold the tambourine with one hand and tap it with the other. See if he can play the tambourine in time to the rhyme 'Pat-a-cake, pat-a-cake, baker's man...'.

kitchen symphony

from 18 months

- Gather different-sized saucepans, some with lids, bowls and utensils such as a large metal spoon, a whisk and a wooden spoon.

- Play some classical music and show your toddler how to beat an upturned saucepan or saucepan with lid in time to it.

- Put some dried pasta, whole walnuts or coins into a ceramic bowl or saucepan. Your child can stir this to make a tinkling sound in time to the music.

- Bang two saucepan lids together at dramatic points in the music. Allow your child to experiment with this new instrument.

- Allow him to create his own 'symphony' by playing the different instruments in time to the classical music.

When you are working in the kitchen, these ideas will keep your toddler happy and improve his reasoning skills.

RESEARCH SAYS

‘ Musical activities that focus on rhythm skills, such as tapping out the beat of a song while singing, can improve spelling ability later on. ’

soft shoe shuffle
from 18 months

- Give your toddler two large, empty matchboxes and show her how to rub the rough sides gently together to make an interesting sound.

- Together, sing one of her favourite songs and encourage her to rub the matchboxes together in time to the rhythm. Discuss what the sound reminds her of: 'Does it sound like scuffling feet? Or shuffling slippers?'

- Have her copy you as you take shuffling steps and listen together to how this sounds.

- Now sing her favourite song again, while she plays the matchboxes in time to it and takes shuffling steps.

Help your child to make a simple instrument using matchboxes.

let's sing about it
from 2 years

Helping your child to compose her own lyrics develops her imagination and creativity.

- Choose a repetitious tune your child knows well and ask her to suggest words to describe what is happening at the time. Then say 'Those are good words!' and ask 'Would you like to sing about that?' Accompany your song with the most convenient noises or 'instrument'.

- For example, to the tune of *The Wheels on The Bus* you might sing: 'The peas in my mouth are popping and popping... Now I'm chewing and chewing my chicken...' and so on. (Here, the 'instruments' are eating noises.) If you are out, you might sing: 'Now we are driving and driving along...' and so on. (Clapping hands or tapping feet could be your 'instruments'.)

♫ performer
from 2 years

- If there is a song your toddler can sing by herself, ask her to sing it while you record this on a childproof tape recorder.

- Show your child how to rewind the tape. Then say 'Let's listen to your performance now!' Show her how to press the 'play' button.

- Tell her how much you enjoyed her singing and encourage her to sing the song again, either faster or slower.

- Help her rewind, playback and listen.

- Encourage your child to sing and record other songs.

This activity helps to improve your child's self-esteem, persistence, fine motor skills, and maths- and reading-related abilities.

RESEARCH SAYS

❝ First-year pupils were taught folk songs with an emphasis on melody and rhythm. At the end of the year, and a year later, their reading scores were substantially higher than those of children who did not receive this instruction. ❞

♫ tubular tootings

from 18 months

Making simple instruments is a good way to introduce your child to their different names.

- Collect some different-sized cardboard tubes. Say 'Look! We have some horns to blow!'

- Let your toddler hold each one and hum or 'toot' a tune as he pretends to play. Show him how different wind instruments are held – 'This is a flute' (holding a tube horizontally out to one side); 'This is a clarinet' (tube held vertically); 'And this is a trumpet' (tube held straight out in front).

- Say 'Let's play our flutes (clarinets, trumpets)!' Have him copy your placement of the instrument and finger actions. Toot or hum melodies together.

- Produce interesting noises: tie some plastic wrap tightly over the tops of your 'horns', place your lips lightly against it and blow. The sounds will vary, depending on the sizes of your tubes.

RESEARCH SAYS

‘ In one brain imaging study, musicians who began their musical training before the age of 7 were found to have brains that differed noticeably in structure compared to non-musicians. The part of the brain that links the two halves of the brain was larger in musicians. ’

♫ hey diddle, diddle
from 18 months

If you accompany familiar nursery rhymes with actions, your child's attention is automatically secured.

- Teach your toddler the nursery rhyme *Hey Diddle, Diddle*, and talk about the illustrations to it in a book.

- Act out the rhyme by pretending to play a 'fiddle', then jumping 'over the moon', then laughing like the 'little dog' and then running away hand in hand.

- Now make some 'instruments'. Place an elastic band around a cereal box to hold a wooden spoon on it, the handle extending off one end. Use another wooden spoon as the 'bow' for this 'fiddle'. Use a plastic plate and another spoon as a drum and drumstick.

- Now sing the rhyme together – one of you 'plays' your new fiddle while the other beats the 'drum'.

♫ drums for all
from 2 years

Encouraging your child to play a drum in time to music enhances automatic balance and motor co-ordination, a prerequisite to tackling more complex tasks.

- Help your toddler make a snare drum from a cardboard egg carton and some string. Give him two paintbrushes as drumsticks. Hang the drum around his neck so that it rests horizontally against his tummy. Then hum or play some band-type music and march together as he beats his drum in time to it.

- Using a cardboard hat box or plastic laundry basket, help him create a 'jungle' drum. Then hum or play some jungle music, and have your toddler sit cross-legged on the ground and play the drum with a wooden spoon.

- You can make drums for pop or symphony concerts.

♫ water music
from 18 months

- Collect plastic bottles of different sizes and shapes, with lids screwed on loosely.

- Fill a large plastic tub with water. Then see if your toddler can unscrew the lids and fill the bottles with different amounts of water.

- Help him screw the lids on again tightly, then listen to the sounds made by shaking the different bottles.

- Now play some music on tape or CD. Choose a bottle each and shake it in time to the music.

- See if he can play two water shakers at once, and accompany both fast and slow music in time to the beat.

You may not stay very dry during this activity, but it will yield benefits for your child's analytical thinking.

♫ spicy music
from 2 years

Your child will be intrigued by the wide variety of sounds that can be produced by changing the contents of a jar.

- Collect some clear herb/spice jars with lids. These are ideal for tiny hands. Help your child fill each jar with a different noise-maker – beans, peppercorns, rice, lentils. Tighten the lids and listen to the sound each makes.

- Ask your child to place three 'shakers' in a row. Tell him to close his eyes and listen to each one in turn. Then shake one of the three and see if he can guess which one it was. Let him test your listening abilities in a similar way.

- Have him choose his favourite shaker and play it in time to different kinds of music.

♫ musical chairs
from 2 years

- Make a circle with small cushions or chairs and place a musical instrument (toy or homemade) on each one.

- Ask your child to choose an instrument, then show him how to walk around the circle playing it.

- Say 'Well done! Can you do that in time to this music?' Then play some music on tape or CD.

- After a minute, turn off the music and say 'You are so good at that! This time, listen for when the music stops and see if you can stop, too! Remember – as soon as it stops, stop walking and stop playing. Are you ready?'

- Give him several practices at this. Eventually, tell him that he stopped brilliantly.

- Tell him he can exchange his instrument for a new one – the one on the nearest cushion or chair.

- Continue the game in this way.

This game is a great opportunity for your toddler to play an instrument in time to music.

RESEARCH SAYS

❛ Evidence suggests that playing music enhances brain development more than just listening to it. ❜

♫ parade
from 18 months

Playing an instrument while moving is a complex task for young children and stimulates the neural circuits in many regions of the brain.

- Collect toy band instruments that are light enough to carry around – bells, shakers, trumpet-shaped party whistles or horns, or homemade drums.

- Say to your toddler 'Let's go on a parade!' Then each choose an instrument.

- Play some band-type music with a pronounced beat and march around together, playing your instruments in time to it.

- Then change instruments and play again, or change the music and see if your toddler can keep time to this.

RESEARCH SAYS

‘ **Music-making stimulates the development of neural pathways in the brain that are involved in reasoning, creative thinking, decision-making and problem-solving.** ’

♫ swell bells
from 2 years

This problem-solving activity is ideal for budding scientists.

- Set out three tall glasses (with sturdy bases) in a row. Help your child to make a bell-like noise by striking (not too hard!) one of the glasses with a metal teaspoon.

- Help her discover that the edge, not the bottom of the spoon, sounds best. A loose grip also gives a clearer sound. If the glass is struck near the rim, not the base, the sound is more bell-like.

- Adjust the water level in each glass so that she can produce a low 'daddy' sound, a middle 'mummy' sound and a high 'baby' sound.

- Make up different 'songs' by varying the order and the number of times she strikes each 'bell'.

♫ comb & tissue tickle
from 2 years

This activity is an especially useful way to improve reasoning and fine motor skills.

- Show your child how to make a simple 'mouth organ' with tissue paper and a plastic comb.

- Fold the paper around the comb and ask her to put the instrument in her mouth and blow gently. Ask how her lips feel when she blows: 'Do they tickle?'

- Take turns playing music for each other, replacing the tissue paper. While one person plays, the other dances a 'tickly' dance on tiptoes in time to the music.

- Vary the speed and rhythm of the music, so that your child performs different dances on tiptoes.

♫ matchbox magic
from 2 years

- Fill the matchboxes with tiny biscuits, currants or sultanas.

- Help your child make two or three shakers. Then sing favourite songs and nursery rhymes, and see if she can shake her shaker in time to them.

- Then see if she can dance around in a circle while singing and playing her shaker at the same time.

Small matchboxes make ideal shakers. Make sure that the contents are safe for toddlers to eat.

♫ snippity-snap
from 2 years

Ballpoint pens with clicking tops make excellent pretend instruments and are useful tools for accelerating fine-motor skills.

- Find two pens like this and show your child how to make a clicking sound.

- Say 'Can you do this?' Make two clicks with your pen and congratulate her ability to copy you.

- Gradually challenge her to copy more and more complex click sequences.

- Your child may also enjoy giving you sequences to copy – occasionally make errors to see if your child notices.

- Think of things that make clicking sounds and then sing to the tune of *The Wheels on The Bus*: 'The switch on the lamp goes snippity-snap, snippity-snap, snippity-snap...; The wheels on the train go clickety-clack...'. See if your child can make the right sequence of clicks to the words 'snippity-snap (clickety-clack)' – three quick ones followed by a slow one.

♫ rattlesnake

from 2 years

- Acquaint your child with the concept of a rattlesnake. You could look at picture books or visit the zoo.

- Say 'Let's be rattlesnakes! We need to make some rattling tails.' Help your toddler tie rustling or jingling objects with pipe cleaners to a length of coloured chenille (or string) at intervals. Use small bells, curtain rings, pieces of foil or small matchboxes filled with peppercorns.

- Teach your toddler this song to the tune of *I'm a Little Teapot*: 'I'm a little rattlesnake, Long and thin, Here is my rattle, And here is my grin; When I get excited, I make a din! Here comes my bite! Sharp like a pin!'

- Pin your tails to your trousers or skirt and perform actions in time to your singing: wiggle and squirm along the ground, hold up your rattle and shake it, display a large grin, shake your rattlesnake tail again, and bare your fangs (teeth) and pretend to bite, chasing after each other.

This make-believe game will increase your child's overall intellectual and creative talents.

RESEARCH SAYS

❝ Singing lessons and group music play have been shown to boost the creative thinking and motor skills of 3- and 4-year-olds.' ❞

music all around

Listening and responding to all types of music.

Music has been shown to greatly benefit childhood development both intellectually and socially, and most children love to sing or play an instrument. Listening and responding to all types of music will improve your toddler's language and listening skills and is a fantastic way for children to interact socially whether by dancing in a group or making music together.

♫ ready, steady
from 18 months

- During day-to-day activities, play music on a sound system or tape recorder, so that your toddler begins to associate an activity with a particular kind of music.

- During any of these sessions, clap your hands, tap your toes, shake a rattle or play an instrument in time to the music that is playing.

- Encourage your child to join in. See how long he can keep a steady beat. He may find this easier with particular kinds of music.

- Try alternating claps, where you clap your own hands and then each other's. Attempt to maintain a steady beat throughout.

This activity is designed to improve your toddler's overall brain functioning.

♫ all kinds of music
from 18 months

By exposing your child to a wide variety of music, you stimulate regions of the brain responsible for spatial, verbal, balance, memory and other skills.

- Play different kinds of music for your toddler. Let him respond in whatever way he chooses – by dancing, singing, humming, or playing with his toys more calmly or with more concentration than before.

- Try to expose him to classical music, pop, jazz, opera, nursery rhymes, country and western, marching tunes, and Asian music. Watch his reactions and you will soon learn what kind of music he prefers.

- Tell him the name of his favourite composer (song, band, album, type of music). He may request it by name. Be sure to praise his excellent memory.

♫ same or different?

from 2 years

- Sit with your back to your child and say 'I am going to make two noises.' Then make two identical sounds (whistles, coughs, claps, clicks, squeaks, kisses) separated by a few seconds. Ask 'Those two noises were the *same*, weren't they? Listen again. Can you tell me if these two noises are the *same*?'

- Make two new identical noises, asking 'Were those two noises the *same*? Did they sound the *same*?' When your child understands, tell him how clever he is.

- Now make two varying noises. See if your child can tell that they were *different*. If not, show him how you made the noises, so he can see that you had to do something different to produce each one.

- Continue making noises that are the *same* or *different*, encouraging your child to use these words.

Your child's ability to discriminate sounds will be improved by playing this game.

RESEARCH SAYS

❝ Listening to music has physical effects on the body that can affect a child's emotional state, stress and activity levels, and his sensitivity towards others. In one study, the presence of background music increased the number of social interactions among children. ❞

♫ if you're happy

from 18 months

This singing activity is an excellent way to expand your toddler's vocabulary, as the possibilities for lyrics are almost endless.

- Young children love the song *If You're Happy and You Know It*.

- Sing the first part, substituting different words: 'If you're happy (sleepy, hungry, cross, tiny, huge, thirsty, washing, sneezing, an airplane, a bus, a train...) and you know it...' Then stop and ask 'What are you going to do?'

- See if your toddler can suggest an action to perform, then sing this version of the song together, performing the new actions.

- If he is unable to suggest anything, ask questions like: 'Should we go and lie down? Nibble on this biscuit? Have a hug?'

- You could also help give him ideas by singing alternate verses, where you sing responses such as: 'When I'm warm and friendly I give you a kiss (hug, cuddle); When I'm hot and bothered I wash my face (go and lie down, wave my arms); When I'm curious about something I ask questions (read a book, scratch my head...)'

RESEARCH SAYS

❛ Music instruction that includes listening, visual and motor activities can improve reading ability. ❜

♫ sharp ears
from 2 years

This listening game helps build your child's auditory discrimination skill, as well as his thinking and reasoning abilities.

- Sit your child in a large, comfortable chair. Go behind the chair and ask him to listen carefully. Explain that you are going to 'play' two pieces of music. Say 'But sometimes it is very difficult for me to think of two pieces of music that are not just the same. Here are two pieces of music. Listen to see if they are the *same* or *different*.'

- Continue with 'Here's the first music', then clap once. 'And here's the second music', then clap twice. Ask 'Were they the *same*? Was the second music the *same* as the first music?'

- Begin with very simple rhythms and your child will soon be able to make high-level listening decisions!

♫ DJ dancer
from 2 years

By giving your child some control over the music he wants to listen to, you enhance his self-esteem, listening and critical thinking skills.

- Let your child have control over the station dial on a radio. Challenge him to find some music he likes. When he does, dance together in time to the beat.

- Then, let him find another station with music he likes. Clap together in time to the beat.

- For the next piece of music he finds, hum along together in accompaniment. For the next piece, sway to the music without moving your feet.

- You can also play this game by showing your toddler how to select different tracks on a CD.

♫ copycat
from 18 months

- Sit facing your toddler and say 'Your ears are looking pretty sharp today. I bet they can hear anything! Shall we make some music together? Can you do this?'

- Then clap a very simple rhythm – perhaps two claps separated by a few seconds.

- Then ask 'Can you do that?' Gradually make the series of claps more complex – two slow claps followed by three quick claps, four quick claps followed by two slow ones, and so on.

- Encourage your child to copy you, repeating any rhythms that need more practice. Give plenty of praise for good copying.

This is another auditory discrimination and memory game.

♫ beat that!
from 2 years

This game is targeted at improving your child's auditory memory, which is fundamental to virtually all learning.

- Show your child a toy (or homemade) drum or tambourine and let her play randomly with it. Then ask 'Would you like to play what I play?'

- Tap out a simple rhythm for your toddler to listen to.

- Ask 'Can you play that?' See if your child can copy the rhythm you made, giving her help and praise.

- Start with very simple rhythms – perhaps just two taps. Then try two quick taps followed by one slow tap, and so on. Eventually your toddler might create simple rhythms for you to copy.

♫ one, two or three?

from 2 years

- Sit your toddler beside you in front of a keyboard instrument (toy or real). Play one note and ask your child to play one. Then ask 'How many notes did I play? How many notes did you play?' Praise your child if she answers correctly both times. Otherwise, repeat the exercise.

- Then ask 'Shall we play two notes now?' Then play any two notes. Encourage your child to copy you by playing any two notes.

- Ask 'How many notes did you play that time? And how many did I play?' Act very pleased if she answers 'Two!' Teach the concept of 'three' in the same way and then play this game.

- Say to your toddler 'Close your eyes. How many notes can your ears hear?

- Then play one, two or three notes. Ask your child to open her eyes and tell you how many notes she heard: 'One, two or three?'

Research reveals that early keyboard instruction – the focus of this game – enhances brain development in a variety of ways.

RESEARCH SAYS

6 Musical instruction can improve both reading and maths skills. After underperforming primary school students were given musical instruction, they caught up with average pupils in reading and were ahead in maths. 9

♫ where has it gone?
from 2 years

This singing game will improve your child's visual memory.

- Put three small objects (sock, comb, toy car, teaspoon, toothbrush, eggcup) on a large plastic plate or tray and show them to your toddler. Ask her to name each object and if she does not know one, name it for her.

- Through discussion, ensure that she says the name of each object herself at least twice. Ask her to close her eyes and name the three objects. Then say 'Please wait there while I take this away for a minute' and carry the plate away. Out of view, remove one of the items.

- Return and say 'I'm afraid I was so hungry I've taken one of the things away to eat! Do you know which one?'

- Take turns testing each other. On returning with the plate, the player sings to the tune of *Oh Where, Oh Where Has My Little Dog Gone?*: 'Oh dear! Oh dear! Which one is gone? I wonder which one it can be...?'

RESEARCH SAYS

❛ **In boys, the left side of the brain seems to handle the lyrics of a song while the right side is more involved in remembering melody. In girls, both sides of the brain tend to be involved in both these processes.** ❜

♫ do you know the name?

from 2 years

One-on-one conversations are the best way to accelerate your toddler's language development.

- To the tune of *Do You Know the Muffin Man*, sing to your child 'Do you know the name of this, the name of this, the name of this?... (repeat)... Tell me if you can.'

- Point to a body part or an object. Or, to elicit a verb from your child, act out something such as combing hair, brushing teeth or driving a vehicle.

- Help her sing in response: 'Oh yes I know the name of that, the name of that, the name of that... (repeat)... That is called a _____ (That is known as _____).'

AA rhyming games

from 2 years

Finger-plays can be adapted to become rhyming action games that will help to develop your child's sense of rhythm, rhyme, balance and tempo.

- You and your child can make up games together, but here are some suggestions to get you started.

- 'Round and round the racing track... (run around in a large circle side by side with your toddler) Like a racing car, One zoom, two zooms... (take two large, lunging jumps) And look where we are! (dive to the ground crashing into one another).'

- 'Round and round the garden... (prance around together in large circles) Like a tabby cat, One step, two steps... (stop and take two prancing steps) And a pounce like that! (pounce on your child as if catching a mouse).'

♫ keyboard copy
from 2 years

- Place your toddler beside you in front of a piano, electric keyboard or organ (toy or real). Say 'Look at your clever little fingers. Are they ready to play?' Let her experiment, pressing the keys as she likes.

- Then say 'Let's play a game! Do you think you can do what I do?' Play one note on the keyboard and see if your child can play that same note.

- Next, play two notes that are side by side on the keyboard. Use the same finger for each note. See if your toddler can copy you. Progress to three notes, all of them side by side, using one finger only. Later, show her how to use more than one finger, progressing to three notes (three fingers) or more.

A musical keyboard activity helps to develop the spatial reasoning abilities that underlie maths and science.

♫ who came first?
from 2 years

This game helps improve your child's ability to discriminate pitch.

- Hold up your little finger and say 'This is Little. This is the sound he makes.' Then hum a very high note. Hold up your thumb and say 'This is Big. Here is the sound he makes.' Then hum a very low note.

- Now say 'Oh! Big and Little both want to talk,' and hum a high note followed by a low note. Ask 'Who came first – Big or Little?' If necessary, repeat the notes.

- Then say 'Oh! Big and Little both want to talk again,' and this time hum the low note followed by the very high one. Ask again 'Who came first?' Continue with other pairs of high and low notes.

dressing the part

from 2 years

- Gather some props for you and your child to use when listening to different kinds of music.

- Dress in cowboy hats and boots, play some country and western music, and dance in that style – hands on hips and clap your hands.

- Dress in shoes that are too large and some silly hats; make your noses red. Play some circus music and behave like clowns – do somersaults and pull hats over each other's eyes. Try to move in time to the music.

- Dress formally in bow ties, play some classical music and let your child take part in a 'concert', playing along in time to the music on a keyboard instrument (toy or real).

Make-believe and fantasy games like this accelerate the development of many cognitive abilities.

RESEARCH SAYS

‘ **Three-year-olds given piano keyboard training developed spatial abilities that were 34 per cent better than another group of children who had been trained for the same amount of time in computer keyboard skills.** ’

♫ mood music

from 2 years

Encouraging children to respond to music can improve vocabulary, emotional and motor abilities.

- Gather a selection of music to encourage different emotional responses from your child, for example: happy, sad, grumpy, sleepy or silly.

- Play some happy-sounding music and say to your child 'Does this music sound happy? Does it make you feel like smiling?' Then smile at each other. Ask 'Does it make you feel like dancing?' Then dance together.

- After a few minutes, play some sad-sounding music and ask 'How does this music sound to you? It doesn't sound so happy, does it? Does it make you feel sad?' Make sad faces at each other.

- Ask 'Does it make you feel like crying?' Pretend to weep, wiping your eyes. Continue the game in this way.

RESEARCH SAYS

❛ Children as young as 3 years are good at detecting the emotional mood of a piece of music. They can match happy or sad cartoon faces with various kinds of music played to them quite accurately. ❜

♫ leap frog
from 18 months

A child of this age probably enjoys musical activities most when they involve movement, as in this game.

- To the tune of *Mary Had a Little Lamb*, sing 'Little frogs like to leap, leap, leap, leap, leap, leap; Little frogs like to leap, leap, leap; That's what frogs like to do.'

- One player curls up small like a frog and the other player 'leaps' (climbs) over. Then the first player climbs over, and so on. Sing the song together several times.

- Then ask 'What do rabbits do?' 'Leap' as before, while singing: 'Little rabbits like to hop, hop, hop...'. Perform any other 'leaping' verses you can think of.

- Change the actions for 'Little snakes like to slither and slide...', and 'Little birds like to fly, fly, fly...'.

♫ ride a white horse
from 2 years

This singing game is a fun way to speed your child's intellectual development.

- One player is the horse and the other the rider. Dress the horse in a white cloth and attach some 'reins' (a long ribbon around back of the neck and under the arms). Attach bells to the rider's toes and tie rings made of string around one finger of each hand. Attach metal bangles to these rings.

- Horse and rider now gallop off singing *Ride a Cock Horse*: 'Ride a white horse to Banbury Cross, I'm a fine lady upon (gentleman on) a white horse, With rings on my fingers and bells on my toes, I shall have music wherever I go!' Try singing at different speeds, the 'horse' adjusting its actions accordingly.

the hunting trip
from 2 years

- Begin with 'Let's go and hunt bears! Are you ready? OK, put your feet on the road like this and here we go!' (Place one hand on each knee; children copy.) 'Here we go, walk, walk, walk, walking down the road.' (Pat one knee, then the other, in a steady rhythm.)

- Then ask 'What's that ahead?' (Put hand to brow and look puzzled; children copy.) 'Oh! It's a river. Have to swim it! What do we have to do?' (Children repeat and copy your swimming actions.) Then say 'Back on the road again!' (Children repeat and resume knee patting.)

- Carry on like this, encountering 'obstacles' along the way. Finally, having asked what's ahead, you say 'It's a BEAR!' Start 'running' (pat knees much faster) and repeat all the actions rapidly in reverse order, saying: 'Back on the road!' and so on, until 'Home at last!'

This story activity, where children copy your actions, is fun to play with a group.

sing & point
from 2 years

This game combines singing with actions and brings many benefits, both physical and intellectual.

- To the tune of *Oh Where, Oh Where Has My Little Dog Gone?* take turns singing these verses to each other:

- You sing 'Oh where, oh where is mummy's (daddy's) nose (knee, toe...)? Oh, where, oh where, can it be?' Continue singing until your child locates and points to the part of your body you named.

- She then sings 'Oh where, oh where is (her name)'s chin (neck, elbow, thumb...)? Oh where, oh where, can it be?' You then point to the part of her body that she named. Continue taking turns to sing your questions.

♫ naughty notes
from 2 years

- Play one note in a series on a toy piano, keyboard, xylophone, guitar or other musical instrument.

- Tell your child that all the notes sounded the same because you played the same note each time. Play the sequence again for her to listen to.

- Ask her 'Do all the notes sound the same? Or did a naughty note creep in?'

- Take turns being the 'listener' and the 'player', so that your child will have a chance both to listen and to devise a series of notes for you to listen to.

This odd-one-out game is an excellent way to train auditory skills.

RESEARCH SAYS

❝ Early experience with songs, sung by loving parents, helps build neural networks in the brain involved with social-emotional development. ❞

numbers

and logic

introduction

Your preschool child is learning something new every day. Sharing the pleasure of early learning with your child is exciting for you both, and even the simplest of activities can be used to introduce new concepts, such as shapes, counting and patterns.

When you try out the games and activities in this book, be guided by your child's mood. Choose a time when she's happy and relaxed. A good tip for capturing her interest is to start playing a game by yourself – an activity that's already underway can often tempt your child to join in. Don't be afraid to go back to games that you've played before – children learn a lot through repetition.

This section is packed with games and activities that will captivate your child and teach her all about the world of numbers and logic. Many of the skills she learns will help her with maths and reading in the future. Counting and Numbers looks at first counting games and number recognition. You may want to keep returning to this chapter, as numeracy skills develop over time and your child's level of understanding increases each time she plays a game. Children under three shouldn't play with small items, such as counters or dice, as there's a risk of choking. So be extra vigilant if younger brothers or sisters are playing alongside your preschool child.

Weighing and Measuring is full of activities, with lots of practical experiments to enjoy.

everyday counting

Here are some examples of the counting activities that you and your child can do in the course of one day:

- Slowly count aloud while you get your child dressed – a useful distraction if she's keen on running off!

- Count the stairs as you go down to breakfast, the fingers of toast on her plate and the number of mugs on the table.

- Outside, count the number of houses before you turn the corner of your street, the number of letters to post and the number of dogs you pass.

- In the shops, count how many apples are in the bag or how many yogurts are in the pack.

- In the bath, count your child's ears, eyes, fingers and toes.

Below: Working through an exercise together provides enjoyment for both you and your child.

Below left: Music fires up a child's imagination and promotes a sense of well-being.

useful things to buy or collect

- Adhesive dots
- Card
- Children's glue
- Children's scissors
- Counters
- Felt-tip pens
- Finger paints
- Large crayons
- Large-squared paper
- Lined paper
- Modelling dough and shape cutters
- Old magazines for cutting up
- Paper fasteners
- Paper plates

- Peg board and pegs
- Plain paper
- Plastic model animals (for example, farm, zoo and sea animals and dinosaurs)
- Playing cards
- Poster paints
- Ribbon, string or wool
- Shape templates
- Sticky paper shapes
- Toy money
- Tracing paper
- Two dice
- Wooden bricks (different shapes, colours and sizes)

Many focus on cooking in the kitchen and water play, so it's essential to supervise your child whenever she is near potential dangers, such as knives or a hot oven. Never leave a young child alone with water.

Your child can have great fun comparing herself to the world around her in Shapes and Sizes. Young children are fascinated by shapes, and love the chance to show you that they recognize them. Once your child has grasped a knowledge of shapes and sizes she can use them to play the games in Patterns and Sequences.

You can improve your child's observation and memory skills with the games in Sorting and Matching, many of which can be played with everyday objects in your home. Anticipating what might happen next is a vital life skill, and the

games in Guess Ahead give your child practice in making logical predictions.

Spotting what's wrong with words or pictures also involves sophisticated logical thinking, so What's Wrong? is full of silly scenarios where your child has to identify the deliberate mistake – not always as easy as it might seem!

In Musical Games, the book concludes with a selection of activities that include numbers and counting – children often find numbers easier to remember when they appear in a song or a rhyme and it also makes learning more enjoyable.

Developing confidence with numbers and logical skills gives your child a real head-start for school and adult life, so we hope you enjoy the activities together. Above all, have fun!

counting and numbers

Little children love to count, even though they don't know what the numbers mean at first.

The games in this chapter help children learn to count up to five, up to ten and then back down again. There are also activities to encourage children to recognize written numbers.

toys' teatime
from 3 years

This teatime picnic game is a great way to introduce your child to counting.

- Choose two toys for a picnic tea.

- Lay out a toy tea-set and ask your child to give herself and each toy one cup, one saucer and one plate. Describe what she's doing: 'One for teddy, one for rabbit and one for you'.

- Make some mini-sandwiches and ask her to give each toy two sandwiches, talking through her actions.

- Do the same with other finger foods.

- Now help the toys enjoy their tea!

RESEARCH SAYS

❝ **Teaching your child to count shows her how to group things according to whether they are alike or different. Children absorb information best when it is presented in a fun, practical way, like counting everyday objects.** ❞

how many spots?

from 3 years

Drawing spots on ladybirds brings a visual dimension to counting.

- Draw several outlines of ladybirds.
- Colour them red together with your child.
- Now ask your child how many spots she thinks the first ladybird should have (five or less). Use a black pen to draw on the spots and then write the number alongside.
- Take it in turns to decide how many spots the second, and subsequent ladybirds, should have, and then draw them on.
- An older child can draw on her own spots and write her own numbers, perhaps by tracing over a faint line that you have drawn.

number story

from 3 years

Using numbers within a story can make them more meaningful to your child.

- Start with, 'Once upon a time there was a pretty bird who sat all alone on her empty nest'.
- 'One morning the bird looked into her nest and was very surprised to see one tiny egg lying on the twigs.' Hold up one finger or draw a nest containing one egg.
- 'The next morning the bird looked down again and was even more surprised to see another tiny egg lying on the twigs. She counted up her eggs: one, two.' Hold up two fingers or add another egg to the nest.
- Continue until the bird has five eggs in her nest.
- Finish by saying, 'One morning the pretty bird heard some cheeping ... and, looking down into her nest, she saw five hungry little chicks just waiting for their dinner!'

which one has six?

from 4 years

This game encourages accuracy in counting.

- Divide a piece of paper into four sections.
- Draw three balls in the first section, six boats in the second section, four flowers in the third section and two fish in the fourth section.
- Together with your child, count the number of objects in each section and ask her to point to the one that contains six.
- Make the game harder for your child by increasing the number of choices.
- An older child can draw extra objects so that all of the sections contain six items.

lucky throw

from 4 years

Using a die helps your child to recognize patterns of numbers.

- Show your child a die and explain how each side shows a different number of dots from one to six.
- Take turns to throw the die and count how many dots are showing.
- When your child is confident with this, get another die and throw together to see who gets the highest number.
- See how many throws it takes until you both get the same number.
- An older child can try counting both sets of dots on the dice.

match mine
from 3 years

Can your child count out the same number of objects as you?

- Find a range of small objects, such as counters, bricks, buttons or beads. Give half of each to your child and keep half for yourself.
- Put down two bricks, counting them out as you do so. Ask your child to put down a button beside each brick.
- Gradually increase the number of objects you put down and get your child to match that number (using a different object). You can also swap so that your child goes first and you match her number of objects.
- If your child finds this game difficult, suggest she puts each one of her items exactly next to each one of yours.

RESEARCH SAYS

❝There are two elements to counting: recognizing the sound of an individual number and its written symbol, and linking this to a specific quantity of objects. It is putting the two together that is difficult.❞

houses in a row

from 3 years

Making a concertina street may help your child to recognize written numbers.

- Take a strip of paper and fold it into a concertinaed square. Before you unfold the paper, make a diagonal cut from halfway up each side towards the centre at the top. Now unfold the paper to reveal a series of house shapes joined together.

- Ask your child to draw a big door on each house. Then write on the door numbers. Count how many houses there are, pointing to the door numbers as you go.

- Ask your child to decorate the doors and houses, then put them on the fridge with magnets, or make a hole at each end and hang them up.

RESEARCH SAYS

❛Children learn well when matching the words 'one', 'two', 'three' to a sequence of objects. Encouraging your child to point to each object and count in this way will facilitate his learning.❜

animal extras

from 4 years

Drawing different size groups of objects helps young children to remember numbers.

- Draw a kitten with three balls of wool beside it. Ask your child how many balls of wool the kitten has to play with.

- Draw a horse with five apples beside it. How many has it got to eat?

- Draw a dog and tell your child you're going to give the dog six bones. Ask him to count the bones as you draw, and to stop you when you've drawn enough.

- If your child finds this easy, ask him to draw the objects for animals himself: four carrots for a rabbit, seven eggs for a hen or ten twigs for a bird's nest.

match the pictures

from 4 years

Help your child to practise his counting skills by getting him to link matching sets of objects.

- Draw six circles. Draw four apples in one circle and four pencils in another (not too near the first circle). Draw two more matching circle pairs (for example, five oranges and buttons, and seven books and balloons).

- Ask your child to draw lines joining the circles that contain the same number of objects.

- Repeat this game, adding an extra circle of objects that doesn't have a matching partner. Ask your child if he can spot the odd one out.

number dominoes
from 4 years

Playing dominoes is a great way to get your child excited about numbers.

- Cut out 28 cards of 8 x 4 cm (3 x 1.5 in). Draw a line down the middle of each card to create two squares. On the first seven cards put one dot on each left-hand square. On each right-hand square, put dots from one to seven.

- On the next six cards put two dots on each left-hand square. On the right-hand square, put dots from two to seven. Continue to reduce the cards by one each time. Your final card should have seven dots in each square.

- Shuffle the completed cards. Give yourself and your child eight each and put the remainder in a pile.

- Lay down the first card. Your child must match the number of dots at either end of your card with one of his own. If he can't, he must take a card from the pile. Then it's your turn. The first person to use up all their cards wins.

race me!
from 4 years

This first board game is a fun way to encourage your child to count up to six.

- Draw a wiggly path of two fairly wide parallel lines.

- Divide the path into 50 or so squares. Make the first square the starting point, the last the finishing post, and number the others in between.

- Add some lucky moves, such as, 'You've landed on a treasure trove, move on two squares', and some unlucky moves, such as, 'There's a rock on the path, go back one square'.

- Put two counters on the starting point and take turns to throw a die, moving the counters as many squares forward as the dots on the die show.

- The first person to the finishing post is the winner.

fruity fractions

from 4½ years

This game is a practical way to introduce your child to the concept of fractions.

- Explain to your child that many objects can be divided into equal portions so that two or more people can share them.

- Cut an apple in half and ask him how many people could have a piece.

- Cut the apple into quarters and ask your child how many people could share it now.

- If your child finds this easy, set out the segments of an orange and ask him to count them.

- Try giving your child a small bunch of grapes and asking him to share it between you so that you each have the same number of grapes.

RESEARCH SAYS

❛Preschoolers only take in two to three objects at a glance (adults take in about seven). More objects must be counted to ascertain how many there are. Objects arranged in specific patterns, such as the dots on dominoes, can help at-a-glance number recognition.❜

up to ten and back

from 4 years

This game encourages your child to use her fingers to count with.

- Using a non-toxic and non-permanent pen, write the numbers one to ten on your child's fingertips. Start with one on her left thumb, moving on to six on the little finger of her right hand and ending with ten on her right thumb.

- Ask her to curl her fingers up in a ball. Start counting and ask her to raise the appropriate finger as you say each number. When you get to ten all her fingers should be showing.

- Now ask your child to fold down each finger as you count back down. When you reach one, all her fingers should be hidden.

RESEARCH SAYS

❝ **When first learning to count, your child chants numbers as she would nursery rhymes – by simple imitation and repetition. To understand a number's meaning, she must learn that five is one more than four and one less than six.** ❞

blast off!
from 3 years

Your child will love the anticipation of counting back from ten as her rocket gets ready to blast off into space.

- Make a rocket from a cardboard tube with a cone of card on top. Let your child decorate it.
- Cut out 11 cards and write a number on each from one to ten, plus the words 'blast off!' on the final card.
- Put the cards in a pile in numerical order with ten on the top and the 'blast off!' card at the bottom.
- Hold the rocket on the floor while your child turns over the cards and counts downwards.
- When she gets to 'blast off!' make the rocket soar up in the air.

one cunning mouse
from 3 years

This simple story is an amusing introduction to the concept of counting down.

'Once upon a time there were five galloping horses.
The five galloping horses were chasing four racing pigs.
The four racing pigs were chasing three speedy dogs.
The three speedy dogs were chasing two fat cats.
The two fat cats were chasing one cunning mouse.
But what happened to that one cunning mouse?
Why, he ran squeak, squeak, squeak, into his hole and
   never came out again!'

- Use finger movements as you count down, and then count how many animals there are altogether.

textured numbers
from 3 years

Decorating a number with bright colours can help your child to remember it.

- Choose a number – your child's age is a good choice – draw its shape on a piece of card and cut it out. The larger the better.

- Scrunch up some brightly coloured tissue paper into small balls.

- Cover one side of the card with children's glue and stick on the tissue paper balls.

- Let the card dry, then punch a hole in the top, thread it with string and hang it in your child's bedroom.

- Repeat with other numbers using a variety of materials for decoration. Make a colour collage from magazine pictures, or use shiny foil, newspaper or cotton wool.

my special numbers
from 4 years

Every child has numbers that are special to him and it's fun to record them in a book.

- Fold over some sheets of paper to make a mini-book. Stick a photograph of your child on the front, then add his name and the words: 'My special numbers'.

- On the first page write: 'I am four years old', making the number larger than the words. Ask your child to colour in the number and draw a picture of himself on the page.

- On the next page write: 'I was born on the ... of ...' (insert the date and month of his birthday), again making the numbers bigger than the words so that your child can decorate them.

- On the next page write: 'My door number is ...', 'Our house has ... bedrooms', 'I have ... soft toys' and so on.

- On the back page write: 'And my favourite number is ...!'.

so tasty!

from 3 years

Edible numbers are not only fun to make (and eat!), they also teach your child what different numbers look like.

- Buy a packet of plain biscuits, a packet of writing icing and some raisins.

- On the first biscuit write the number one in icing. Add another small dollop of icing at the bottom and stick a raisin to it.

- Take another biscuit and write the number two in icing. Stick two raisins underneath.

- Continue like this until you've reached five. Then line all the biscuits up in a row from one to five, ready to eat.

RESEARCH SAYS

‘ **Children have an innate awareness of quantity. Think how upset your child would be if you gave him one cookie less than his friend! When you teach your child about numbers, you are directing this natural interest.** ’

my number frieze
from 3 years

This decorative number frieze makes numbers part of your child's everyday environment.

- Cut out five pieces of card measuring 15 x 20 cm (6 x 8 in).
- Cut out magazine pictures of, for example, one person, two cars, three dogs, four cushions and five plates.
- Write the number one large on the first card and ask your child to stick on the picture of the person. Repeat with the other cards, matching numbers and pictures.
- Put the cards up around your child's bedroom in numerical order. Alternatively, make a book with them.
- Add more number cards when you feel that your child is ready.

spot the number
from 3 years

Focusing on one number helps to clarify it in your child's mind.

- Choose a 'number of the day' and draw it on a piece of card for your child to see and hold.
- During the day point out that number every time you see it: on car licence plates, doors, buses, shops, petrol stations, price labels and so on.
- Surprise your child by cutting out the number from a slice of bread or forming it from some mashed potato. At the end of the day talk about all the different places you saw the number.
- Sing a song or read a bedtime story to your child that involves the number, such as Three Little Pigs or Snow White and the Seven Dwarfs.

mini-bingo

from 4 years

Playing bingo is an exciting way to introduce number matching to your child.

- Cut out two rectangular pieces of card and divide each one into two rows of five squares. In each square write random numbers from one to ten.

- Now make two more boards bearing exactly the same numbers as the first two. Cut this second set up into individual squares and put them in a bag (one that you can't see through).

- Give your child one board and keep the other yourself.

- Take turns to pick a square from the bag. If it matches a number on your board, lay it over the top of that number. If it doesn't, put it back in the bag.

- The first person to cover their board with squares wins and shouts 'bingo!'.

RESEARCH SAYS

6 Showing your child how adults use basic maths helps her to make the connection between the counting games that she plays for fun and the usefulness of applying numbers to everyday life. 9

weighing and measuring

Children enjoy making discoveries about themselves and the world around them.

The weighing and measuring activities in this chapter are hands-on games that use everyday objects. They give your child the opportunity to use numbers in a very practical way. They also encourage observation skills as your child explores the concepts of length, weight and capacity.

pizza maths
from 4 years

Most children love making pizza and it offers lots of opportunities for practical maths.

- Buy a large, ready-made pizza base, tomato purée, grated cheese and a selection of toppings, for example, olives, sliced tomatoes, strips of pepper or pepperami slices.

- Spread the purée on the pizza base and sprinkle with grated cheese.

- Use a knife to lightly score the pizza base into slices.

- Ask your child to add the toppings so that each slice gets an equal amount.

fruity cocktails
from 4 years

This fruit juice cocktail game helps your child to understand the concept of capacity.

- Gather together three clear plastic cups and a measuring jug.

- Decide with your child which juices to mix in your cocktail, for example, orange, apple and cranberry.

- Pour a small amount of orange juice into one cup, apple juice into the second, and cranberry in the third. Now ask your child to complete the cocktail by adding roughly equal amounts of the other juices to each cup.

- Let your child pour the three drinks into the jug, first guessing how far up the jug the cocktail will come.

- For an older child, vary the amounts of juice you put in each cup, using a measuring jug for accuracy.

let's make cakes

from 4 years

Your child learns about weighing and measuring with this simple fairy cake recipe – but make sure she stays away from the hot oven!

- Gather together eggs, sugar, flour and butter.
- Ask your child to weigh 60 g (approximately 2 oz) of each ingredient. Alternatively, let a single egg be their measuring guide – crack it into a measuring jug, check the level, then measure the same amount each of sugar, flour and butter.
- Cream together the butter and sugar with a wooden spoon. Mix in the egg a little at a time. Then add the flour gradually.
- Spoon the mixture into cake cases, and bake in a medium oven for 12–15 minutes.
- An older child may be able to suggest what would happen if she used too much or too little of any of the ingredients.

RESEARCH SAYS

❛Activities such as baking provide valuable lessons not just about weights and measures but also about breaking a task down into stages that must be performed in a set sequence (children don't naturally look at activities in terms of sequences).❜

funny feet

from 4 years

Teach your child a fun way to measure things using his own feet.

- Ask your child to stand without shoes on a piece of paper or card.
- Draw round the outline of his feet and help him to cut out the shapes.
- Ask your child to use the cut-out feet to measure familiar objects, such as a table – how many steps can the feet make across the surface?
- Use the feet to measure longer distances, such as the width of a room or the garden.
- A younger child will enjoy making lots of feet and placing them end-to-end, where you can number them and help him to count them.

that's me!

from 4 years

Help your child to learn about length and numbers using his own body.

- Use a large piece of paper, such as wallpaper, to draw around the outline of your child's body.
- Look at the outline together and ask your child whether his arms are longer or shorter than his legs, and how many fingers and toes he has.
- Ask your child to draw in his eyes, nose, mouth and hair, then clothes (including buttons).
- Count your child's features together and describe how eyes, ears, arms and legs come in pairs, whereas we have only one nose and mouth.
- Help your child cut out the outline of his body and stick it on his bedroom wall.

how tall am I?

from 4 years

Your child will love making first discoveries about his height.

- Find a ball of wool and a pair of child-safe scissors.
- Ask your child to stand up straight by a wall or lie on the floor. Tuck the loose end of the wool under his heel, or tape it down.
- Unravel the wool until it's at the top of your child's head. Cut it so that you have a piece that's the same height as your child.
- Encourage your child to use the wool to compare his height with other things in your home such as the height of a door or chest of drawers, the width of a stair or the length of his bed.

RESEARCH SAYS

❝ Central to your child's understanding of numbers is the discovery that things can be 'bigger than' or 'smaller than', 'taller than' or 'shorter than'. Measuring familiar objects using an improvised ruler facilitates this discovery. ❞

giant in the garden

from 3 years

This game uses imaginative ways to measure an area of floor or ground.

- Tell your child that you're both giants who take enormous footsteps.

- Count how many giant steps it takes you to get across the living room floor or garden.

- Now you're going to be dainty pixies who take little skipping steps. How many steps does it take this time?

- Next try being frogs or rabbits who have to hop, or birds taking pigeon steps.

- Count out loud together as you go.

- To vary the game, mark out a large circle with string, and see how many steps or hops it takes to get around your circle.

RESEARCH SAYS

'Children find it difficult to hold more than one comparison in mind at a time. Tasks that involve looking at the sizes of several items at once encourage your child to make multiple comparisons.'

a neater bookshelf
from 3 years

This useful activity encourages your child to arrange objects in height order.

- Tell your child that you're both going to tidy up her bookshelves.
- Look at the shelves and ask your child to point out the tallest and the shortest books.
- Help your child to re-order the books so they're all in height order.
- Congratulate her on having a neat and tidy bookshelf!

house hunt
from 4 years

A tour of your home helps your child to make visual comparisons of room sizes.

- Pretend that you and your child are explorers, setting off to discover things about where you live.
- Ask your child to lead you to the smallest room and then to the biggest room in your house.
- Ask your child to take you to the narrowest part of your house.
- Are there any rooms that are taller than others?
- Now count how many rooms, doors and windows there are in your house.
- An older child may enjoy preparing a list of things to look out for, and ticking them off as she goes.

the great wall
from 4 years

This easy building game encourages first counting skills.

- Gather together your child's bricks – the more the better.
- Ask him to build a wall that stretches all the way across his room, or if you have enough bricks, all the way around his room.
- Count how many bricks there are in the wall by marking off groups of ten.
- Alternatively, build a shorter wall with several rows of bricks, and count up how many rows there are.

up the stairs
from 3 years

This activity demonstrates how height can be increased in easy steps.

- Find 40 square construction bricks. Help your child to build a square base measuring four by four bricks.
- Add another layer of bricks to the base but miss out a row to create a stair.
- Add another layer of bricks but miss out two rows to create a second stair. Finally, add just one row of bricks to create a third stair.
- Ask your child to help one of his toys climb the steps, counting them as he goes.
- An older child may enjoy making a tall, narrow staircase only two bricks wide but ten bricks long.

toy parade

from 3 years

Your child will love spotting the differences between his favourite toys.

- Gather together a selection of your child's toys at random.
- Ask him to pick out any two of them and put them side by side.
- Now ask him to tell you which one is bigger and which one is taller or longer.
- If he has lots of toys of one particular type, such as teddies or cars, ask him to line them up in order of size.
- Alternatively, help him to sort all his toys into groups – soft toys, cars, puzzles and so on – and then count how many there are in each group.

RESEARCH SAYS

❛ Large groups of objects are difficult for your child to quantify because he cannot see at a glance how many there are. Dividing objects into smaller groups makes counting and comparing activities more manageable. ❜

splish, splash, splosh
from 3 years

Pouring water is a fun way for children to learn about how liquids are contained.

- Your child can play this game in the bath, at the sink or with a large bowl of water. Stay with your child all the time he's playing with water.
- Give him a selection of things he can use for pouring water: a small plastic jug, a beaker, a yogurt pot with a small hole in the bottom, a sieve, a funnel and a small plastic bottle.
- Ask your child which things hold water and which let it pass through. Talk about how quickly or slowly the water passes through the objects with holes in them.
- An older child may enjoy finding out how many times he can fill up a small beaker with the water from one plastic bottle.

RESEARCH SAYS

6 Young children find it hard to grasp how liquids occupy spaces. Until around the age of six, if shown a tall glass and a short glass, each containing an equal amount of water, they will always believe that the tall glass holds more water. 9

which has more?
from 4½ years

This is a quick way to introduce your child to the fascinating properties of liquids and the concept of volume.

- Find a measuring jug and two transparent cups – one that's short and wide, the other tall and narrow.
- Pour 100 ml (3.5 fl oz) of water or juice into the measuring jug, and show your child the mark the liquid has reached on the side of the jug.
- Pour the liquid into the short cup.
- Measure out another 100 ml (3.5 fl oz) of liquid and pour this into the tall cup.
- Put the cups side by side and ask your child if he thinks one contains more than the other, or if they're both the same.

it's pouring!
from 3 years

Play this game to discover the different rates at which solids and liquids can be poured.

- Collect a number of household ingredients such as salt, rice and dried lentils, and pour equal portions into plastic cups.
- Add cups of water and dry play-sand to your collection.
- Ask your child to pour each item in turn through a funnel, colander, sieve or a plastic pot with a hole in the bottom.
- Talk about how water pours very quickly, followed by salt and sand, and then rice and lentils. Do any of the ingredients get stuck? What happens if the ingredients get wet?
- An older child can use a timer – you can help him to record his findings on paper.

roundabout
from 4 years

This is a simple introduction to the idea of measuring solid objects.

- Help your child to cut a piece of string around 15–20 cm (6–8 in) long.

- Collect a selection of objects, such as an orange, a jar, a book, a small box and a beaker.

- Ask your child to compare how far the string will go round each one.

- He can also try measuring your wrist and ankle and comparing them to his own.

who's the ruler?
from 3 years

Your child will enjoy making independent observations and using a grown-up tool.

- Show your child a short ruler.

- Send him on a mission to find three things that are longer than the ruler, for example, a cushion, a soft toy and a box of cereal.

- Next he has to find three things that are shorter than the ruler, for example, a teaspoon, an apple and a CD.

- Point out other household objects and ask him to discover if they're longer or shorter than the ruler.

wiggly jiggly
from 4 years

This simple measuring activity helps your child to understand that objects of the same length can look very different.

- Cut two equal lengths of ribbon. Arrange one in a wiggly line and the other in a straight line.

- Ask your child which of the two pieces of ribbon he thinks is the longest.

- Straighten the wiggly piece of ribbon to show him that both pieces of ribbon are the same length. Let your child repeat the exercise by himself.

- Try making other shapes, such as circles, coils, squares or triangles with the pieces of ribbon.

RESEARCH SAYS

❝ Research suggests children do not have a concept of measurement until they learn to put things into sequences, for example small, medium, large. Try to do these tasks systematically because this will help them to understand. ❞

weigh it up
from 3 years

This is a hands-on way to discover weights and measures.

- Gather a variety of small items from around the house or garden, making sure that some are heavier than others.
- Ask your child to become a human weighing scale, simply by holding her hands out to the sides.
- Place a light object, such as a leaf, in one palm.
- Place a heavier object, such as a pebble, in the other palm.
- Ask your child to judge which is the heavier item.
- This game also works well if your child closes her eyes so she has no visual clues as to which object is heavier or lighter.

RESEARCH SAYS

❛Some mental comparisons can't be made until your child has developed an appropriate level of memory. When this level is reached, you can help her to practise her comparison skills by encouraging her to make lots of visual comparisons of objects at home and outdoors.❜

park life
from 3 years

An outing can encourage your child to use her powers of observation to judge weights.

- Go for a walk in the park with your child.
- If there's a pond, ask her if she can see which duck looks like the biggest and heaviest. Are there any smaller or lighter birds?
- Look at the plants and trees. Ask your child to find something that's very light, such as a twig, or to point out something that's very heavy, such as a tree.
- Look out for animals and birds in the trees. Are they light or heavy? What would happen to a thin branch if a big animal climbed on it?
- Pick up a stick and ask your child to bring you something that's heavier and something that's lighter.

let's get together
from 4 years

This game reinforces your child's understanding of how weights vary.

- Draw a line down the centre of a piece of paper.
- On either side of the line draw some heavy things, such as a lorry, an elephant and a hippo, and some light things, such as a pin, a feather and a bubble.
- Ask your child to draw lines that connect pairs of light things and pairs of heavy things.
- Ask your child if she can think of any more especially heavy or light things, and then draw pictures of them together.

shapes
and sizes

Shapes are a key concept in maths, but as far as your child is concerned they're just lots of fun.

With your encouragement he'll quickly learn to recognize and name basic shapes, and will find shapes such as stars and hearts fascinating. When he starts to learn about size, he will enjoy making comparisons that relate directly to himself – whether he is bigger or smaller, taller or shorter than other people in your family!

where's the square?
from 4 years

Play this game to stimulate your child's visual memory of shapes.

- Draw, colour and cut out a circle, a square, a triangle and a rectangle.

- Line them up and show them to your child.

- Explain that you're going to take one of the shapes away. Ask her to close her eyes and take away the square.

- Push the remaining shapes together, then ask your child to open her eyes and tell you which shape is missing.

- Play the game again, taking away a different shape. You can make the game easier by using fewer shapes, or more difficult by adding more complex shapes such as diamonds, pentagons and hexagons.

making shapes
from 4½ years

This shape-making activity helps your child to understand how many sides shapes have and that not all shapes have sides of equal length.

- Cut out a selection of thin paper strips, making most of equal length and a few shorter or longer.

- Show your child how to make a square from four pieces of paper that are equal in length. See if she can make one without help.

- Ask her to make a rectangle from two long and two short pieces of paper.

- Ask her to make a triangle, first from three pieces of paper that are equal in length and then from three pieces of different lengths.

- Can she make a diamond or even a pentagon?

- Point out which shapes you can't make with straight sides, such as a circle or an oval.

shaping up
from 3 years

Children find it immensely satisfying to create their own simple shapes.

- Using soft modelling dough, help your child to roll out a long, thin sausage.
- Show her how to form a circle by joining the ends of the sausage together.
- Next, make the sausage into a triangle or a square.
- If your child finds this difficult, draw the shapes clearly on a piece of paper, and ask her to place the modelling-dough sausage over your outlines.
- Once she's confident, try more complicated shapes such as a diamond or star.
- An older child will enjoy counting how many sides each shape has, or even measuring and comparing the length of each side.

RESEARCH SAYS

6 **A two-year-old is unlikely to be able to match a three-dimensional shape with a two-dimensional one, such as a sphere with a circle. Even at the age of three, this task is difficult and will need a lot of practice.** 9

big square

from 4 years

This simple game shows your child how joining shapes together can create new ones.

- Gather together some square and triangular bricks.
- Ask your child to fit four square bricks together. Describe how he's created one big square from four small ones.
- Ask your child to add more square bricks around the perimeter to make an even bigger square.
- Set an older child the challenge of making a small square from two triangular bricks or a bigger one from eight. See if he can make a rectangle from six square bricks. Which bricks – and how many – does it take to make a house shape with a triangular roof?

RESEARCH SAYS

❝ Learning about shapes and objects is more complex than it might seem. Your child may be able to point out a rectangle and a book but he will have difficulty grasping the concept that the book is also a rectangle. ❞

match the brick
from 3 years

**Help your child
to recognize
identical objects
by size, shape
and colour.**

- Gather an assortment of different shaped bricks.
- Choose a cube and hold it up for your child to look at.
- Ask your child to find a brick that is identical in terms of shape, size and colour.
- Give him clues such as 'its sides are all the same size', or 'this one looks like an arch'.
- Make the game easier or harder by limiting or extending the choice of bricks.

pick a brick
from 3 years

**Encourage your
child to explore
the different
properties of
three-dimensional
shapes.**

- Empty a box of mixed bricks on to the floor.
- Ask your child to pick out three or four bricks.
- Experiment with each one to discover what it can do. Can you roll it along the floor? Can you stack it on top of anything else? Can you put anything on top of it? Can you slide a pencil underneath?
- Point out any surprises, for example, cylinders can't be stacked on their sides, but when they're upright you can pile them high.

colour my shape
from 3 years

This game helps your child to identify shapes, even when they're of different sizes.

- Draw a selection of circles, squares and triangles of the same size. Find some crayons or coloured pencils.

- Choose a colour and/or pattern for each shape, for example, red spots for circles, blue stripes for squares and green zig-zags for triangles.

- Ask your child to colour the shapes in the appropriate colours and/or patterns.

- Now draw the same shapes but in different sizes. Ask your child to colour them in again.

- To make the game easier for younger children, draw each shape in a row.

paper snowflakes
from 4 years

This creative activity teaches your child how to make a range of complex shapes and designs by folding and cutting paper.

- Cut out a circle of paper, then count aloud 'one, two, three, four' as you fold it over four times to make a fan shape.

- Using child-safe scissors, show your child how to make snips in the top edge and down either side of the fan.

- Let him open up the paper. Point out how the snips have created a snowflake shape.

- Ask him to make several snowflakes and compare the designs of each one.

picture this

from 3 years

This activity will help to improve your child's confidence at recognizing shapes.

- Look at a picture from a magazine or a picture book.
- Ask your child if he can spot any familiar shapes within the picture, for example, square windows, a circular wheel or a rectangular table.
- Count how many there are of each shape.
- Draw a picture of your house and see how many familiar shapes you can include.
- Try and draw a picture using only one shape, for example, a robot drawn from only squares.

RESEARCH SAYS

❛Pointing out shapes within a picture is difficult for small children. For example, your child may be able to point out the petals on a picture of a flower but unable to point out anything that is oval-shaped.❜

can you feel it?
from 4½ years

Children love this very physical way of learning to sense shapes.

- Explain that you're going to trace the outline of a shape on your child's palm.

- Ask her to close her eyes and hold out her hand. Lightly trace a circle.

- If she can't guess what the shape is, let her watch while you trace the circle again.

- Try tracing other shapes. Vary the game by tracing a shape on your child's back. Or let her keep her eyes open while you draw the shape in the air.

RESEARCH SAYS

❛ Learning to recognize shapes in drawing and shape-sorting games helps your child to recognize letters and words and is a valuable pre-reading skill. ❜

double up

from 3 years

Encourage your child to observe shapes carefully by copying your pictures.

- Cut out some simple shapes from coloured paper.
- Make a picture out of the shapes. For example, a tree from a rectangle and a triangle, or a house from a square with a triangle on top.
- Ask your child if she can copy the picture you've made, using identical shapes.
- If this is difficult, give her the appropriate shapes to get her started. If it's easy, get her to make a picture for you to copy.

picture scene

from 4 years

This exercise encourages your child to build imaginative pictures from familiar shapes.

- Cut out an assortment of shapes from coloured paper or use ready-made gummed shapes.
- Show your child how to stick the shapes on to paper to create a picture.
- Ask her to make a boat from triangles, a house from squares or a flower from circles.
- Now ask her to make pictures from multiple shapes. Encourage your child to create a background to her picture. Together, count how many shapes she has used.

where's my baby?

from 3 years

This favourite theme of 'mothers and babies' helps your child learn about size and number.

- On a piece of paper draw simple pictures of a cow, sheep, fish, horse and chicken.
- Somewhere else on the paper, draw the baby animals that belong to each creature.
- Ask your child to draw a line connecting each baby to its mother. Who is bigger – the mother or the baby?
- To make it more challenging, include animals with 'unusual' babies, such as butterflies and caterpillars, or frogs and tadpoles.
- Count how many animals there are altogether.

sizewise!

from 3½ years

This fun activity helps your child to understand height and age differences between people.

- Draw simple pictures of your family or friends that reflect their respective heights.
- Help your child to cut out the pictures, then lay them in a row and count them.
- Ask your child if he can put them in height order. Help him by asking, 'Who is the tallest? Who comes next? Who is the smallest?'.
- Alternatively, arrange the family in age order. Has anyone moved places?
- Let your child colour in the pictures and stick them down.
- He will also enjoy playing this game with cut-out animals or plants and trees.

who's hungriest?

from 4 years

Familiar themes, such as dinner time, make it easy for your child to understand the concept of small and large portions.

- Draw two big plates and one small plate in a row on a piece of paper. Alternatively, use paper plates.

- The first plate is for dad, the second is for mum and the third is for your child.

- Ask your child to draw some sausages on each plate. The first plate should have three sausages, the second should have two and the third should have one.

- Now ask your child to draw a large, medium and small portion of chips and peas on the respective plates.

RESEARCH SAYS

❝ **Children's drawings give us a fascinating insight into how they see the world. Even when your child masters shape, the relative sizes of the flowers and the house tell us that there is still much to learn.** ❞

busy caterpillar

from 3 years

Encourage shape recognition and counting with this simple but satisfying exercise.

- Draw eight to ten circles on a piece of card, cut them out and help your child to colour them in a variety of bright shades.

- Draw a face on the first circle and help your child to stick it on a large piece of paper. Add antennae.

- Stick the other circles on to the piece of paper so that they overlap in a wiggly line.

- Draw two legs on each circle.

- Help your child count how many circles make up the caterpillar, and how many legs it has altogether.

busy box

from 4 years

This activity shows your child that it's possible to create a 3-D box from a 2-D shape.

- Draw four fairly large squares of the same size in a straight line on a piece of card. Draw an extra square on either side of the second square in the line. You now have a cross shape.

- Cut out the cross shape, fold the creases, then use a hole-punch to make a hole on each side of the four outermost squares.

- Fold the squares so that they form a box with a lid.

- Help your child thread a piece of ribbon or wool through the holes.

- Put a small treat, treasure or toy inside the box and then tie the ribbon to keep it safe.

six sides

from 4½ years

Challenge your child by letting him experiment with more complex shapes.

- Cut out a hexagon (a shape with six equal sides) from a piece of card. Draw round the hexagon ten times on a piece of paper.

- Ask your child to colour each hexagon a different colour and then to cut them out carefully.

- Ask him to make different patterns with the hexagons by fitting them together in a honeycomb.

- Make more hexagons but this time ask your child to cut each hexagon into triangular sections like cake slices and colour each one differently. Count how many triangles there are in each hexagon.

RESEARCH SAYS

6 Understanding how shapes tessellate, or the difference between shapes of different dimensions, are important maths skills. Although girls equal or surpass boys in maths tests, more boys than girls have precocious mathematical ability. 9

watch me grow

from 3 years

Play this fantasy game in which your child imagines growing from a tiny seed into a tall tree.

- Ask your child to curl up on the floor and pretend that she is a tiny seed.

- Tell her that the sun is shining and the rain is falling on her. It's time to uncurl – ask her to stand up very slowly and stretch her arms towards the sky. When she is upright, tell your child to imagine that she is a big, strong tree.

- Repeat the exercise but pretend that your child is a chick hatching out of an egg and growing into a chicken.

- Talk to your child about how sizes change and how babies get bigger as they get older. Show her something that she can reach now that she couldn't reach when she was smaller, such as a door handle.

hands and feet

from 4½ years

This game shows your child how the area of your hand holds more than hers.

- Help your child to draw round her hand on large-squared paper. Then draw round your own hand on another piece.

- Count how many whole squares fall within the outline of her hand and how many in yours. Which hand has the most?

- Ask your child to colour in all the whole squares in one colour, and the partial squares in another colour.

- Try the same experiment with your and your child's foot.

I'm a star!

from 3 years

Making shapes with her body is a novel way to help your child to visualize and remember them.

- Tell your child she's amazingly bendy and can make herself into almost any shape she likes.

- Stand in front of a mirror and ask your child to become a star with her arms above her head and her feet positioned wide apart.

- Now ask her to be a ball by crouching down and tucking her head between her knees.

- Now ask her to make the shape of a pencil by standing up as straight and tall as she can.

- Finally, ask her to become a triangle shape by bending forward and putting her hands flat on the floor so that her body forms a wide 'v'.

RESEARCH SAYS

6 **Different styles of learning suit different children. Some children respond best to sitting down and working with pencils and paper; others prefer physical activity, exploring the world of space, size and shape with their bodies.** 9

patterns and sequences

Understanding patterns and sequences is fun for your child and helps him to make sense of the world.

Patterns are all around us, from those in the natural world, such as the markings on a zebra, to the patterns in the man-made world, such as road markings, brickwork or the decorative patterns used in art and design. These activities will help your child to identify some of them.

which colour next?

from 3 years

Teach your child about simple alternating patterns using toy bricks.

- Gather a selection of same-sized bricks in two different colours, for example, red and yellow.

- Start a row of red bricks then ask your child to finish the row by adding more red bricks. Do the same with a row of yellow bricks.

- Now make a row using alternating yellow and red bricks. Say the names of the colours as you lay them down, 'red, yellow, red, yellow', and so on.

- Give your child a red and a yellow brick and ask him to choose which one he thinks should go next. If he finds this easy, let him finish the row.

RESEARCH SAYS

❛ **Children find it hard to understand that sometimes activities or objects need to follow on after each other in an ordered way. Sequences of two things, such as two differently coloured bricks, are a good introduction to this idea.** ❜

fingerprint rows
from 3 years

This simple painting exercise is a great way to introduce your child to the concept of pattern.

- Choose three different colours of children's paint.
- Dip your child's finger into one colour and help him to make a row of fingerprints.
- Wipe his finger and let him dip it in the second colour. Make a second row of fingerprints.
- Make a third row of fingerprints with the third colour.
- Make a fourth row of fingerprints with the first colour. Keep repeating the rows of fingerprints until the whole page is filled to make a pattern.

colour squares
from 3 years

Show your child how to create a diagonal pattern of colour using a square grid.

- Draw a grid consisting of 16 squares (four down and four across).
- Select four coloured pencils and colour each square in the top row a different colour, for example, yellow, red, blue and green.
- Colour in the second row of squares, but this time move each colour along one square, for example, green, yellow, red, blue.
- Do the same with the next two rows, moving the colours along one square each time.
- Show your child the diagonal patterns of colour that you've made.

repeating shapes
from 4 years

Can your child guess which shape comes next in the sequence?

- Draw an alternating pattern of two shapes, such as a circle and a rectangle. Say the names of the shapes as you draw them.
- Stop just before you get to a rectangle and ask your child if he can guess which shape you are going to draw next.
- If he finds this difficult, go through the row again pointing out the pattern.
- If he finds this easy, let him finish drawing the row.
- Make the pattern more complex by using three shapes.

animal patterns
from 4 years

Making a chart of animal spots and stripes enhances your child's awareness of patterns in nature.

- Draw two columns on a large piece of paper. One is for spots and one is for stripes.
- In the spots column draw or ask your child to stick in pictures of creatures that have spots, such as a ladybird, leopard, jaguar or butterfly.
- In the stripes column draw or stick in pictures of creatures that have stripes, such as a tiger, bee, wasp, caterpillar or zebra.
- Which column has the most animals?
- Talk about other patterns and markings that you see on animals and insects.

print magic
from 3 years

Making potato prints is a fun and traditional way to learn about shape and pattern.

- Cut a potato in half and sculpt a raised square on one half and a raised triangle on the other. Alternatively, cut cross-sections of a carrot.

- Help your child to dip the potato square into some thick paint, then press it down on the top left-hand corner of the paper. Repeat the print across the top of the paper.

- Dip the potato triangle into a different colour and make a row of triangles underneath the squares.

- Continue alternating rows of squares and triangles until your child has covered the paper.

RESEARCH SAYS

6 **Children classify objects on the basis of a single feature. When introducing the idea of sequences to a child, it's a good idea to present sequences in which only one feature varies, such as shape, colour or size.** 9

build with counters
from 4½ years

How many patterns can your child make from six counters?

- Lay six counters in a row and count them together with your child.

- Rearrange the counters in two rows of three. Count them again.

- Now make the counters into a tower and count them.

- Finally, make a pyramid with three counters in the bottom row, two in the middle and one on top. Count them again.

- Repeat this exercise with different numbers of counters. Which numbers make even rows? Which make pyramids? Which numbers will do both? How many counters do you need to make a square?

RESEARCH SAYS

❝ **Counting is not a skill exclusive to humans; animals count too. If lions hear the roar of one lion, they go out to face the enemy, but if they hear three different lions roaring they lie low.** ❞

how many legs?

from 4 years

This animal-naming game helps your child to understand that legs come in pairs.

- Ask your child to name creatures that have two legs, for example, a bird, duck, monkey or person.

- Ask him to think of four-legged creatures, for example, a cow, horse, cat or dog.

- Ask him to think of six-legged creatures, for example, a beetle, ladybird, grasshopper or bee.

- Ask him to think of eight-legged creatures, for example, a spider or octopus.

- Point out that all the animals he has named have pairs of legs. Ask him which creature has too many legs to count. A centipede!

one to one hundred

from 4½ years

A hundred-square grid is useful for recognizing many different sorts of number patterns.

- Draw a grid of ten squares by ten squares. Ask your child to make each row a different colour.

- Starting from the top left, write the numbers one to ten along the top row.

- On the second row write the numbers 11 to 20. And so on up to one hundred.

- Point out how each new group of ten starts on a new line and how numbers form patterns. Ask him to draw a line through all the numbers with zero or five in.

- Make this grid on a computer so that you can print out several copies. Use them for colouring in different patterns, such as multiplication tables.

adding on one
from 4 years

This activity is a first introduction to simple addition.

- When your child can count up to ten ask him if he can tell you 'what's one more than one?'.

- If he can, keep going up: 'what's one more than two?', 'what's one more than three?', and so on. Demonstrate with real objects.

- When he's confident, pick numbers under ten at random.

- Eventually, move on to numbers up to 20. Once they grasp the general idea, older children will be able to manage quite large numbers.

making ten
from 4½ years

Teaching your child which pairs of numbers add up to ten is a vital first maths skill.

- Count out ten counters or buttons with your child.

- Lay them in a row then move one counter to the side. Show your child that the one counter plus the nine counters still make ten. Let him count them to make sure and then repeat the exercise himself.

- Lay the counters in a row of ten and move two to the side. Show your child that the two counters plus the eight counters still make ten.

- Repeat with three and seven, four and six, and five and five counters.

missing numbers

from 4½ years

Spotting the missing number in a sequence is often harder than it seems.

- Write a row of numbers from one to ten, but leave one number out. Read the numbers aloud and ask your child if he can name the missing one.

- If he finds this difficult, draw several rows of oranges, starting with one orange at the top, then two underneath, then three and so on. Miss out a row and ask him if he can guess how many oranges should be in it.

- Throw a ball back and forth – you count odd numbers and your child counts even numbers. Tell your child to shout if you miss out one of your numbers.

- Older children can spot missing numbers in more complicated sequences such as: 10, 20, 30, ..., 50 or 5, 10, 15, ..., 25, ...

RESEARCH SAYS

❝A child will perceive two evenly spaced rows of counters as containing the same amount, even if they don't. This is because he doesn't yet understand the principle of numerical equality and relies instead on visual impressions.❞

hands up!
from 3 years

Use the five fingers on your child's hand to practise counting in fives.

- Mix up some runny paint.
- Show your child how to dip her hand in paint and press it down firmly as many times as she can on a large sheet of paper.
- Let the paint dry, then write the numbers one to five across the fingers of each hand print.
- For older children, use your hand poster to talk about the idea of counting in fives, for example, two hands have ten fingers, three hands have fifteen fingers, and so on.

animal ark
from 3 years

Putting pairs of model animals into an ark gives your child a practical understanding of what it means to count in twos.

- Gather some model animals and show your child how to pair them up.
- Ask your child to create a line of paired-up animals.
- Improvise an ark from a large upturned hat or box and count the animals in, saying 'two elephants, two giraffes, two zebras', and so on.
- An older child could count the animals in twos: 'two, four, six, eight, ten', and so on.

at the toy shop
from 3 years

Playing shops is an excellent introduction to counting with money.

- Help your child set up a pretend shop with five sections. You could put dolls in one, teddies in the second, bricks in the third and so on.

- Give your child some toy money. Stick to one type of coin of low value.

- Make labels to show how much each toy costs. Write the price and draw the corresponding number of coins next to it.

- Ask her to choose which toy she would like to buy, and help her to count out the number of coins she needs.

- Now it's your child's turn to be the shopkeeper while you choose a toy to buy.

RESEARCH SAYS

❛ **Playing counting games and doing simple sums with your child increases her confidence and shows her that numbers are fun. If she is reluctant to learn about numbers don't push her – you can always try again another time.** ❜

watch the clock!

from 4½ years

A child who is confident with numbers up to 12 may be ready to start telling the time.

- Using a paper plate, draw a large clock face with the numbers clearly marked around the edge. Cut out card hands for the clock and attach them to the face with a paper fastener. Alternatively, use a toy clock.

- Put the big hand to 12 o'clock, then gradually move the small hand around the clock face telling your child the time at each new number.

- Now move the small hand to various numbers at random and ask your child if he can guess what time it is.

- Talk about things you might do at different times of the day, for instance at 1 o'clock you have lunch; at 6 o'clock you have dinner; at 7 o'clock you have a bath; and at 8 o'clock you're fast asleep!

RESEARCH SAYS

❝ Whereas adults perceive time in a linear way, children tend to live in the present. It isn't until he reaches the age of three, that your child begins to understand the concept of today, yesterday and tomorrow. ❞

which goes where?

from 4 years

**Help your child
to understand
the cycle of day
and night.**

- Set out two large sheets of paper. Tell your child that one sheet is for day and the other is for night.

- Name various things associated with either day or night, such as sun, breakfast, bicycle, or moon, bed, pyjamas. Ask your child whether each thing belongs to day or night and draw it on the appropriate sheet.

- When both sheets are full, put them up on your child's wall to remind him of the difference between day and night.

how long will it take?

from 4½ years

**Timing how long he
spends on different
activities helps your
child to understand
the passage of time.**

- Using a home-made clock face (see Watch the Clock!) or a toy clock, help your child to count the number of hours he spends doing everyday activities.

- Start by looking at morning activities. If your child spends an hour at playgroup, show him where the clock hands start and finish for this activity.

- Now look at the duration of afternoon activities together. Try to choose activities that last for differing numbers of hours.

- An older child can make a simple chart on squared paper to show how long activities take, using one square for every hour. Discuss which activity takes longest and which is the quickest.

sorting and matching

Sorting objects into groups that share similar characteristics requires careful thinking.

Arranging shapes, putting things in pairs or matching up identical pictures can provide a good foundation for future reading skills. These challenging yet enjoyable activities help improve your child's observational skills and develop his memory.

fruity fun
from 3 years

Sorting fruit into categories of type, colour and shape encourages your child to be aware of different characteristics of familiar objects.

- Put a selection of fruit of different colours and shapes on the table.

- Hold up a banana and ask your child to find you another one. Do the same with the other fruit on the table. Ask your child to name each fruit and say what colour it is.

- Now ask your child to sort the fruit by colour. For example, yellow fruit, such as bananas, lemons and grapefruit, and red fruit, such as strawberries, cherries and red apples.

- Finally, sort the fruit by shape, for example, long fruit such as bananas, and round fruit, such as oranges. You can also sort fruit according to whether it is soft, such as peaches, or hard, such as apples.

where do we live?
from 3 years

This sorting game helps your child to identify animal names and types.

- Put some toy animals on the table.

- Tell your child that one corner of the table is the jungle, another is the farm, another is the sea and the last is the dinosaur swamp. Vary the categories to suit the animals.

- Hold one animal up and say, 'This is a pig. Do you think he lives in the jungle, farm, sea or dinosaur swamp?'

- If your child answers correctly, let him put the animal in the right corner. If not, give him a clue to work it out.

- Do the same with the other animals.

the big toy sort!
from 3 years

A toybox tidy-up can easily be turned into a first sorting game.

- Tip a box of muddled-up toys on to the floor.
- Ask your child to search for one category of toy, for example, play figures, while you look for another, for example, jigsaw pieces.
- When you've both found as many items as you can, put them into their own containers. Start a new search for other categories of toy.
- When all the toys are sorted, ask your child to count how many categories you found. Your child can also divide his toys into sub-categories, for example, vehicles can be sorted into cars, lorries and buses.

RESEARCH SAYS

❛ When learning about classifying objects, your child needs to understand that an object can be grouped in more than one way. For example, an orange can belong to a group of orange objects, spherical objects or a group of fruit. ❜

what's it worth?

from 4½ years

Help your child understand how coins relate to each other by compiling this chart.

- At the top of a piece of paper draw a picture of the lowest-value coin.
- Draw a vertical line down the centre of the paper.
- To the left of the line, draw a picture of the second-lowest-value coin. To the right, draw its equivalent in lowest-value coins.
- Continue like this, with coins rising in value down the left, and equivalent low-value amounts on the right. Don't go too high or it will become confusing.

my money box

from 4½ years

Counting your savings is a very personal way to become familiar with sorting out money!

- Give your child a money box or make one from a small box with a slit cut in the top.
- Give your child some coins and show her how to post them in the slot. Let her feel how the box gets heavier each time more coins are added.
- Add coins regularly over a few days or weeks. When the box is nearly full, let your child open it up and sort all the coins into piles.
- Help your child count up how much each pile is worth, then add them together for the grand total.

rub a coin

from 4 years

Rubbing coins encourages your child to observe patterns and helps her to identify different coins.

- Give your child some coins. Ask your child if she knows the names of any of them. If she doesn't, tell her.

- Ask her to sort the coins into matching groups. Point out that the size of the coin doesn't necessarily indicate its value.

- Choose a coin and place it under a sheet of plain paper.

- Give your child a crayon and tell her to rub firmly on the coin through the paper. As the pattern of the coin emerges, ask her which coin it is.

- When your child has done several coin rubbings, help her to cut them out and line them up beside the real coins, saying their names as you do so.

RESEARCH SAYS

❛ **Playing games with coins provides children with a basic understanding of the sequence of numbers. This is especially true if they use coins to buy treats, as a coin of greater numerical value than another can be used to buy more treats!** ❜

spot the twins

from 3 years

Teach your child to use colour coding to match items.

- Draw three stick girls with triangular skirts and four stick boys wearing shorts.

- Colour each girl's skirt a different colour and three of the boys' shorts in matching colours. Colour the fourth boy's shorts in a completely different colour.

- Ask your child to spot the 'twins' – the stick figures with matching colour clothes.

- Can she point out which stick figure isn't part of a twin?

RESEARCH SAYS

‘ For your child to learn to count properly she needs to match a word, such as 'three', with a quantity, such as three balloons. Games that teach general matching skills develop your child's ability to make associations. ’

dolly's wardrobe
from 3 years

Matching clothes to toys involves comparing sizes, and dressing them requires your child to follow a logical order.

- Choose two or three dolls or teddies of significantly different sizes.
- Find one or more outfits, including socks and/or shoes, to fit each toy.
- Put all the clothes in one pile and the toys in another.
- Ask your child if she can sort out which clothes fit which toy. Now help her to dress her toys. Show her how to put clothes on in the right order, for example, a dress before a coat, and socks before shoes.

pick a shape
from 3 years

Play this game with your child to encourage shape identification and sorting.

- From card, cut out some circles, squares, triangles, rectangles, stars, diamonds and ovals. Cut out the same number of each shape.
- Lay a row of different shapes on the floor. Put the rest in a bag or envelope.
- Ask your child to take a shape out of the envelope and place it beneath its matching one on the floor.
- Now it's your turn. If you pick a shape that's already been put down, replace it in the envelope; if not, lay it on the floor.
- The first person to complete a whole row wins that round. Repeat with another row. Continue until all the shapes are used up.

funny socks
from 3 years

This matching game is similar to Pairs (see page 208) but is fun and easier for younger children.

- Cut out 14 sock outlines from card and arrange them into seven pairs.

- Using a selection of art materials, such as sticky dots, sequins, gold stars, tissue paper and crayons, help your child to decorate each pair of socks in a distinctive way.

- Put all the finished socks face down on a table. Take turns to turn over two socks. If they match, keep them and have another go. If they don't, turn them back over.

- The person with the most sock pairs is the winner.

match the cup
from 4 years

This exercise helps your child to match items using colour and shades of colour.

- Take a piece of paper and draw five different colour cups at the top.

- At the bottom of the paper draw five stick girls with triangular skirts. Colour the skirts in the same five colours, or similar shades, such as lilac and purple, as the cups.

- Ask your child to draw a line that joins each cup to the girl with the same colour skirt.

- Repeat the game but add an extra girl and ask your child if she can spot which girl hasn't got a cup. Can your child draw and colour a cup for her?

muddle and match

from 3 years

Children enjoy
fitting boxes, cups
and saucepans
back together
again, and they
learn to match
shapes in the
process.

- Gather several two-piece items, such as storage boxes
  and lids, a plastic bottle and cap, a saucepan and lid,
  a drinking beaker and top, or the top and bottom of
  a soap dish.

- Separate all the tops from the bottoms and muddle
  them all up on the floor.

- Ask your child to match the pieces that fit together.

RESEARCH SAYS

**❝ It is much easier
for your child to
point out two
objects that are
identical to one
another than
match up items
that don't
resemble each
other in size,
shape or colour.
For example, a
hat and a scarf. ❞**

copy my colours
from 4½ years

It's quite a challenge to copy accurately but this exercise quickly hones your child's counting and observation skills.

- Draw two grids consisting of 16 squares (four down and four across) each.

- Colour a selection of squares at random on the first grid.

- Ask your child to colour in exactly the same squares on the second grid.

- If she finds this difficult, suggest she looks closely at each row in turn. Put a ruler under each row to guide her eye.

RESEARCH SAYS

❛ The ability to notice differences and similarities between objects is a very useful pre-reading skill. If your child is adept at noticing fine details, it will help her to recognize words when she starts learning to read. ❜

identical faces
from 3 years

This activity encourages your child to notice small but significant details in pictures.

- Draw six oval shapes on a piece of paper.
- Make two ovals into identical faces with glasses, a hat and a beard (for example). Make the remaining four ovals into faces that differ from the first two in subtle but important details, such as no beard, or without glasses.
- Show the faces to your child and ask her if she can spot which two faces are exactly the same.
- Vary this game by making the facial details easier or harder to spot.

find my partner
from 4 years

This matching game helps your child to apply the everyday observations he has made about the world around him.

- Take a large piece of paper and fold it down the middle.
- On the left, draw one item from a pair of objects that you might expect to go together, for example, a bowl and spoon, hat and scarf, chair and table or chicken and egg. On the right, lower down, draw the other item of the pair.
- Continue like this with other sets of pairs.
- Ask your child if he can draw a line linking each pair.

snap!
from 4 years

This favourite game is great for improving number recognition skills.

- Shuffle a pack of playing cards and deal it into two halves. Give your child one half and keep the other.
- Put your cards, face down, in front of you. Take turns to turn over your top card and place it, face up, in a new pile in the centre. If it matches the one immediately below it shout 'snap!'.
- The person who shouts 'snap!' first keeps all the cards in the centre pile and adds them, face down, to the bottom of his own pile.
- The first person to collect the whole pack wins.
- A younger child could play this game with a pack of 'snap' picture cards.

pairs
from 4½ years

This card-matching game not only helps your child to recognize numbers, but also improves his memory.

- Shuffle a pack of playing cards and lay each one face down.
- Tell your child to turn over two cards. If they match, he can keep the pair and have another go. If they don't, he must turn them back over in their original position.
- Now it's your turn to do the same.
- Continue like this until all the cards have gone. The winner is the person who has collected the most pairs.
- To make it easier, put out only five or ten pairs of cards.

red or black?

from 3 years

Playing card games is an excellent way to learn about matching and sorting items in different ways, and children love playing with grown-up 'toys'.

- Start by sorting a pack of playing cards into two piles: red cards and black cards.

- Now show your child how he can divide the red pile again into hearts and diamonds, and the black pile into clubs or spades.

- Ask him to find the picture cards in all of the piles.

- An older child will enjoy helping you put the suits in rising numerical order, or sorting out groups of four matching numbers.

RESEARCH SAYS

❝ **As your child's cognitive skills become increasingly sophisticated, he will be able to sort playing cards in an increasing number of ways. At first by colour and then, over time, his sorting ability will extend to number, suit and picture cards as well.** ❞

guess ahead

Your child needs to absorb huge amounts of information in his everyday life.

It's not always easy to filter out what's important and what can safely be ignored. These games all give your child practice in resolving situations that require logical decisions. Most involve active discussion, so allow enough time to talk through the game together.

bobbing along

from 3 years

Predicting what will float and what will sink helps your child to make observations about different objects.

- Fill a sink or bowl with water.
- Ask your child to help you choose a number of household objects, for example, a cork, a sponge, a plastic beaker, a toy boat, a teaspoon, a wooden spoon, a sieve, an apple and a pebble.
- Before dropping each one in the water, ask your child to guess whether it will sink or float and why.

RESEARCH SAYS

6 Children, like adults, base their predictions on practical experience. For example, if every time your child presses a button on a toy, a nursery rhyme plays, he will learn to predict that pressing that button triggers the rhyme. 9

how far can you go?

from 4 years

Making a sensible estimate is a very useful pre-maths skill.

- Ask your child to stand at a starting line, and guess how far he can throw a small soft ball.

- Mark the spot he thinks he can reach, then ask him to throw the ball, and see how close he gets.

- If his original guess was very inaccurate, ask him to guess again, and mark a new spot before getting him to take another throw.

- Other ideas for your child to guess about: how far he can roll a ball along the ground; how far he can hop without putting down his second foot; and how many times you can throw and catch a ball between you without dropping it.

make them grow

from 4½ years

This game offers lots of counting practice and encourages your child to predict what will happen next.

- Draw a simple picture of a tree with five nuts on it. Ask your child to count the nuts.

- Below, draw the same tree with the nuts on the ground beneath it – your child may like to write the numbers by each one if you write them faintly for him first.

- Ask your child what he thinks may happen to the nuts now that they're on the ground.

- A third picture can show the nuts now growing into five little trees growing up in front of the big tree.

- If your child enjoys this game, he could add five little nuts to each of the new young trees.

freeze frame!
from 4 years

This experiment shows your child how water expands when it freezes.

- Explain to your child that you can heat up water by boiling it in a kettle, or make it cold by putting it in the fridge or freezer.

- Find a clear plastic beaker and half fill it with water, marking the level of the water on the outside.

- Put it in the freezer. Ask your child what she thinks might happen to it if it stays in there all night.

- The next morning, show your child how the ice has 'grown' by comparing the level of the ice to the original mark on the beaker. Mark the new level. Can she guess what will happen to the level if you leave the water to defrost?

- You can try this experiment using fruit juice so that your child learns how ice-lollies are made.

a sticky situation
from 3 years

Making a sticky dough is a great way to learn about what can happen when you mix a solid with a liquid.

- Give your child a large bowl containing several tablespoons of flour.

- Encourage your child to run his fingers through the flour. Talk about how soft and dry the flour feels.

- Give her a small cup of water and ask what will happen if she adds it to the flour. Now let her find out. Add the water a little at a time and keep stirring.

- Can she describe what is happening? Point out that flour and water mixed together form a totally new substance.

- When the consistency is right for kneading, help your child to roll it out or add salt to make modelling dough.

- Try the same experiment but starting with water and adding flour gradually. Can your child guess the result?

all mixed up

from 4 years

Give your child a first lesson about what happens when you mix two colours together to make a new one.

- Put some red, yellow, blue and white paint on a palette and give your child an old plate to mix colours on.

- Ask your child to guess what colour she will make if she mixes red and yellow, blue and yellow or white and red. Now let her mix them to find out.

- Experiment by mixing different proportions of the colours, for example, using a tiny amount of red with lots of white.

- Help your child make a chart to show how colours mix to make other ones, for example, red + yellow = orange.

- Talk about colour mixes in everyday life. For example, make a cup of black coffee and ask your child what will happen to the colour if you add milk.

RESEARCH SAYS

❝ **Young children do not think in the same way that adults do. If something changes its appearance, a child will believe that it has changed permanently, for example, water changing into ice. They will not realize that it can become water again.** ❞

mind the gap
from 4 years

Encourage your child to think about the meaning and context of words in this sentence-building exercise.

- Describe a scene to your child, such as, 'It's a wet day and the rain is pouring down'.
- Miss out a word from the next sentence and ask your child to guess what that word might be. For example, 'I must remember to put up my ... '.
- Continue in the same way. For example, 'If I put up my umbrella, I will stay nice and ... '.
- Vary the game with sentences describing everyday activities, such as, 'I wash my hair with ... ', or 'I like to ride my ... in the park'.

what should we do?
from 3 years

This exercise demonstrates to your child that considering consequences in everyday life can help to prevent problems.

- Ask your child the following questions. If she gets the answer right, ask her how she could have prevented the outcome.
- What happens if you don't have a drink all day?
- What happens if you don't dry yourself when you get out of the bath?
- What happens if you leave a cake too long in the oven?
- What happens if you forget to fill the car with petrol?

the deepest puddle

from 4 years

**This puddle tour
helps your child to
develop practical
problem-solving and
measuring skills.**

- Go for a walk with your child after it's been raining. Take a ruler with you or find a stick.

- Talk about how puddles gather in dips in the ground. Ask your child if she can predict which of several puddles is the deepest.

- Ask her to dip her ruler or stick into a puddle. How far does the water come up the ruler in terms of finger-widths?

- Use the ruler or stick to measure the other puddles. Did she guess the deepest one correctly?

RESEARCH SAYS

❝ By monitoring brain activity using scanning equipment, scientists have been able to determine that specific parts of the brain are involved in certain tasks. When people are asked to judge whether one number is bigger than another, a specific area of the brain lights up. ❞

weather report

from 4 years

Watching the weather together teaches your child prediction skills and helps him to plan ahead.

- Each morning look out of the window and ask your child to describe the sky and the weather.

- Can he suggest what might happen later? For example, will it be rainy or sunny?

- What clothes does your child think he should wear? Will he need a change of clothes later?

- Draw simple pictures of the weather on a week-long weather chart.

RESEARCH SAYS

❛ Your child may be able to make simple predictions, for example, if he drops a glass, it will smash. Complex predictions, in which A doesn't always lead to B, may pose more of a challenge. ❜

how many shoes?
from 3 years

This drawing game helps to extend your child's counting ability.

- Draw a picture of a little boy. Ask your child how many shoes the boy needs. Ask him to draw on the shoes.
- Draw a cat. If the cat wore shoes, how many would she need? Ask your child to draw shoes on.
- Do the same with an ant and then a caterpillar (with as many legs as your child can count).

how would I feel?
from 4½ years

This activity encourages your child to think about which emotions are appropriate to which situations.

- Set the scene for several situations that would provoke a strong emotion. For example, 'I'm sitting on a beach in the sunshine with a nice cool drink'. Or, 'I'm standing at a bus stop in the rain and I'm very hungry'.
- Give your children a list of emotions, such as happy, sad, angry or frightened, and ask him which he would feel in each situation.
- Ask your child to make up his own situations that would provoke these feelings.

I've had a letter
from 3 years

This exercise shows your child how to use picture clues to deduce the meaning of a sentence.

- Write a simple letter to your child, describing a few events of the day.

- In each sentence, replace one of the words with a picture clue. For example, 'Then I sat down and read my ... '.

- Read each sentence to your child and see if he can supply the missing word. If not, point the picture clue out to him.

picture treasure hunt
from 4 years

All children love treasure hunts and they learn about following clues in the process.

- Cut out five pieces of card and number them one to five. On the reverse side draw a picture clue, such as a bath, sofa, bed, toy box and chair. Hide the cards around the house in numerical order so that each card leads your child to the location of the next card.

- For younger children, make sure the clue cards are clearly visible in each location.

- Hide a prize in the location shown on the fifth card.

- Send your child on a treasure hunt. Once he has found the prize, lay all five cards out in number order and count them together.

what happens if ... ?

from 3 years

Encourage your child to make logical deductions about what might happen next in a series of practical situations.

- Stand at the sink and let water flow into a bowl. Ask your child what will happen when the water reaches the top of the bowl. What about if you left the plug in the sink?

- Build a tower of bricks and wait until you think it might fall. Ask your child what he thinks will happen if you add one more brick.

- Build a tower of rectangular wooden bricks (stacked in alternate directions in rows of three). Ask your child to remove one brick at a time. In each case ask him what the effect will be.

RESEARCH SAYS

❝ By the age of four, your child is able to search systematically for a single object, but if he is asked to find several objects he will look for them strictly in the order that they are presented to him. ❞

fill in the story

from 4½ years

This game promotes your child's memory and also makes him think about story structure.

- Start telling your child a familiar story.

- When you reach an exciting part of the story, pause and let your child tell you what happens next.

- Your child may find this easier if you choose a story that contains a rhyme or a familiar refrain.

- If he's confident, let him tell the story to you, gently prompting him if he gets stuck.

RESEARCH SAYS

❝ The intelligence of a child at the age of three is not a good predictor of adult intelligence. Measured at the age of four, however, a reliable indication can be given of intelligence later in life. ❞

story scramble
from 4 years

This enjoyable game teaches your child to construct a logical narrative.

- Divide a piece of paper into four sections.
- Draw part of a story on each section. For example, a girl walks along; it starts to rain; she puts up her umbrella; she sees a rainbow.
- Cut the pictures out and put them in the wrong order. Ask your child to put them back in the correct sequence and tell you the story.
- If he finds this difficult, give him a head start by telling him the story first.

how can I escape?
from 4½ years

Build your child's imagination and story-telling ability by asking him to think about escaping from fantasy scenarios.

- Tell your child that he is swimming underwater with a net and a torch when he bumps into a big hungry shark. Ask your child what he would do. Suggest how he might escape.
- Invent other fantasy scenarios. For example, your child is armed only with a balloon, a sandwich and a bottle of water and he is being chased by a lion in the jungle or a snake in the desert.

what's wrong?

Children get huge satisfaction and a boost to their confidence when they get things right.

You can have lots of fun by setting up situations where there's a deliberate mistake for your child to identify and correct. The games in this chapter include visual as well as verbal activities that will help your child exercise her powers of logical thinking. And you can laugh about the silly scenarios you create together.

what's in the way?

from 4 years

This imaginary road trip helps your child to come up with his own solutions to practical problems.

- Draw a wiggly road on a large piece of paper, making the road wide enough for a toy car. Draw a house at the end of the road.

- Ask your child to suggest possible hold-ups that could stop the car getting to the house. For example, a fallen tree, a ditch, a flood or a cow standing in the road.

- Draw each of these obstacles on the road.

- Ask your child to push his toy car along the road. As he encounters each obstacle, ask him how he is going to overcome it. If he finds this difficult, suggest your own solutions, such as chopping up the fallen tree, filling in the ditch or hooting the car horn at the cow.

RESEARCH SAYS

❝ Tasks that involve spotting absurdities in pictures, answering questions about how to overcome obstacles, and spotting the odd-one-out in a sequence of items all help to cultivate verbal reasoning. ❞

mind the cars
from 3 years

This fun game helps your child to apply his practical knowledge of transport and how things move.

- Draw some simple outlines of vehicles, missing out an important part in each case. For example, a car or train without wheels, or a plane with a wing missing.
- Ask your child to spot the missing part.
- Draw in the missing part but make it wrong. For example, draw square wheels on a car, or feet on a train.
- Ask your child if he can spot anything wrong. Would the vehicle be able to move?

odd one out
from 4 years

All children enjoy spotting the odd one out and it builds their ability to reason.

- Say a list of words that contains one odd one. For example, 'car, boat, plane, train, egg', or 'cat, dog, horse, glove, sheep'. Ask your child to identify the odd one out.
- If he finds this difficult, give him a clue, or pause just before you say the odd word.
- An older child may enjoy coming up with his own lists, or drawing pictures of the items.

getting around
from 4 years

Teach your child to apply his knowledge about animals and the way they move.

- Talk about the different ways that people and animals move around, such as running, walking and swimming. Ask your child the following questions (or make up your own).

- Which creature is best at flying: a butterfly or an elephant? Easy questions like this will help your child to get the idea of the game.

- Which creature is best at slithering along the ground: a snake or a bear?

- Which creature is best at swimming: a fish or a bird?

- Which creature is best at climbing: a monkey or a dog?

whose house?
from 4 years

This game helps your child to make reasoned judgements about which creatures live where – and why.

- Describe the home of a particular creature and ask your child who he thinks might live there.

- For example, a nest high up in a tree made from twigs and leaves.

- Help your child by giving him a choice of creatures, for example, a dog, a bird or an elephant.

- Talk about how silly it would be, for example, for an elephant or a dog to live in a nest in a tree.

- Ask your child to draw a picture of the correct creature in its home.

animal crackers

from 4 years

Children enjoy the silliness of these mixed-up animals and it gives you an opportunity to talk about how an animal's body is adapted to its environment.

- Choose three animals, and talk with your child about their most obvious characteristics, such as a snake with its long, scaly body; a pig with its snout and curly tail, and a hedgehog with its prickly spines.

- Draw one of the animals but add a wrong characteristic, for example, a snake with hedgehog spines.

- Ask your child to spot what's wrong and to describe what the animal should look like.

- Ask him to draw an accurate picture of the animal.

RESEARCH SAYS

❛ An adult will apply the rules of logic to any given situation but a preschool child will believe what he sees. This is why children find illogical pictures, such as a cat with a bird's wings, very funny. ❜

what's missing?

from 3 years

This drawing game encourages your child to think about the appearance and function of everyday objects.

- Draw a picture of a household item with an important bit missing, for example, a table with only three legs or a teapot without a spout.

- Ask your child what's missing from the picture.

- If she notices straight away, ask her to draw in the missing item.

- If she finds it difficult, offer clues such as, 'Look at each corner of the table'.

- Talk about what would happen to a real table if it only had three legs.

RESEARCH SAYS

❝ **When information enters memory, it may be encoded visually (as a mental picture) or acoustically (as sound). Information such as the layout of a familiar room is encoded visually, whereas a nursery rhyme is encoded acoustically.** ❞

crazy story
from 4 years

Test your child's memory of familiar stories and encourage her to spot mistakes.

- Start telling a familiar story to your child. Ask your child to stop you if she hears anything wrong.
- Introduce a detail that deviates from the usual story, for example, Little Red Riding Hood meeting a cow instead of a wolf on the way to her grandmother's house.
- Ask your child to correct you. Let her continue the story if she wants to.

which room?
from 4 years

This game helps your child to visualize familiar spaces and make reasoned decisions.

- Tell your child that you're going to describe one of the rooms in your house and to shout out 'stop!' if she hears anything wrong.
- Start with an accurate description of your bathroom, for example, and then introduce an anomaly, such as a bed next to the bath or a cooker in the corner.
- If she finds this hard, stop and question her by saying, for example, 'A cooker in the bathroom! Is that right?'.

true or false?

from 4 years

This game teaches your child to differentiate between a true statement and a false one.

- Explain the concepts of true and false to your child and ask him to apply them to the following statements.
- 'Fish like walking along the pavement.'
- 'Monkeys can swing through the trees.'
- 'The sea is pink.'
- You can also use this game to reinforce safety messages, such as, 'It is dangerous to run out in the road without looking'.

my busy day

from 4½ years

Untangling a mixed-up sentence exercises your child's problem-solving skills.

- Talk about the activities you and your child do regularly each day.
- Tell him you're going to mix up two words in a sentence. For example, 'We're going to the ducks to feed the park'. Or, 'Let's go and hair your brush'. Ask him if he can tell you which words have been swapped.
- If he enjoys this, muddle the words even more. For example, 'that squirrel jumping look at!'.

sing-song

from 4 years

Children love nursery rhymes and delight in correcting your deliberate mistakes.

- Start singing a familiar nursery rhyme or song to your child. Ask your child to stop and tell you if he hears anything wrong.

- Introduce a mistake, such as 'Jack and Jill went up the hill to fetch a pail of milk'.

- Ask your child for the correct word or phrase and let him continue to the end if he wants to.

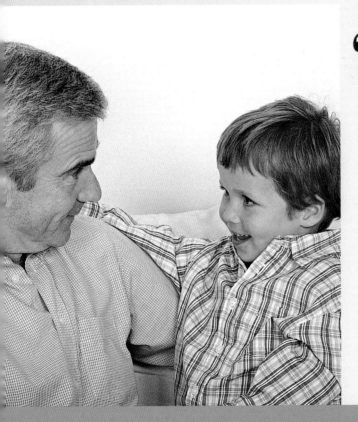

RESEARCH SAYS

‘ **Children are getting cleverer year by year. The average IQ in the UK has risen by 27 points since 1942. Research suggests similar improvements in other European countries, the US and Japan.** ’

spot the difference

from 4 years

This game helps your child to look closely at the details in pictures and to see beyond the obvious similarities.

- Draw simple but identical pictures side by side, such as two fish, two cups and saucers, and two dolls.

- Make two or three minor adjustments to one of each pair, for example, adding some spots and an extra fin to one of the fish.

- Ask your child to look at the two pictures and tell you what are the differences between them.

- If she finds this difficult, offer clues, such as, 'look at the tail'.

- Your child may enjoy adding her own 'differences' to a set of pictures.

RESEARCH SAYS

6 **Concepts simplify and order the world by dividing it into manageable units. Children learn that the concept of an object includes certain properties. They then apply this concept to that 'type' of object, regardless of size, colour or shape.** 9

all dressed up
from 3 years

Sorting her clothes is a practical way for your child to learn about the usefulness of putting things in a logical order.

- Gather some clothes that you would like your child to wear. Ask her to arrange them in the order in which she will put them on.
- Now pretend to put all her clothes on the wrong parts of her body. For example, her trousers on her head and her socks on her hands.
- Ask her if anything is wrong and, if so, to tell you the correct part of her body for each item of clothing.

why doesn't it work?
from 4½ years

These fantasy scenarios will not only make your child laugh, they'll teach her to apply the practical knowledge that she's learned about the world.

- Draw a series of silly scenes and ask your child to spot what is wrong in each case. Can she redraw the scene correctly?
- A man with an umbrella in which the rain is falling underneath the umbrella instead of on top of it.
- A plant growing upside down with its roots in the air and the flower underground.
- A woman wearing glasses on the back of her head.
- A clock with the numbers in the wrong order.
- A sky with stars and a sun.
- A snowman on a sunny beach.

musical games

Pre-school children respond instinctively to nursery rhymes, songs and music.

Children's natural love of music means that it is a great aid to learning. Try these ideas for counting songs, first music-and-movement activities and rhythm and melody games. Listening to music together at any time will provide stimulation and enjoyment.

hammer 'n' count!

from 3 years

The physical actions in this counting rhyme will help your child to remember the numbers.

- Show your child how to make her right hand into a fist and pretend to hammer with it while singing this song:

  'Peter hammers with one hammer, one hammer,
  one hammer.
  Peter hammers with one hammer,
  All day long.'

- Ask your child to make her left hand into a fist as well and sing, 'Peter hammers with two hammers ... '.

- Add an extra hammer in each verse until you get to five (your child can stamp her feet and nod her head for the other hammers).

RESEARCH SAYS

❝ Reading and singing nursery rhymes to your child teaches her not only about rhythm and melody, but also about counting and vocabulary. Children who are read and sung to at home have a head start when they go to school. ❞

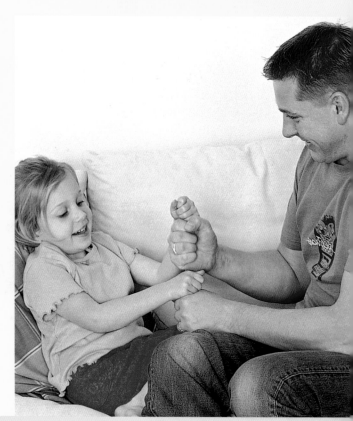

five little ducks

from 3 years

Use this favourite rhyme to help your child practise counting down from five.

- Cut out five duck shapes from a piece of card. Your child can decorate them. Line them up in a row and sing this rhyme, removing one duck when you get to the last line:

  'Five little ducks went swimming one day,
  Over the hills and far away.
  Mummy Duck said "Quack, quack, come back!"
  But only four little ducks swam back.'

- Keep singing the rhyme until there are no more ducks, then make the ducks reappear in the final verse:

  'No little ducks went swimming one day,
  Over the hills and far away.
  Mummy Duck said, "Quack, quack, come back!"
  And all five ducks came swimming right back!'

one, two...

from 4 years

This familiar action rhyme teaches your child to count in twos.

- Act out this rhyme with your child. You can use real props (gather some pencils to use as sticks) or mime the actions.

  'One, two, buckle my shoe.
  Three, four, knock at the door.
  Five, six, pick up sticks.
  Seven, eight, lay them straight.
  Nine, ten, a big fat hen!'

happy song
from 4 years

This adaptation of the well-known song turns counting into a fun activity.

- Act out the following song with your child (the line endings are different from the original version):

  'If you're happy and you know it, clap your hands one time.

  If you're happy and you know it, clap your hands one time.

  If you're happy and you know it, then you surely want to show it,

  If you're happy and you know it, clap your hands one time!'

- In the next three verses change the line endings to, 'wave your arm two times', 'shake your leg three times' and 'nod your head four times'.

RESEARCH SAYS

❝ **Verbal, musical and action memories are stored in three different areas of the brain. This explains why people who experience memory loss and cannot learn a new story may still be able to learn to sing or play a new tune.** ❞

going to the zoo
from 3 years

This game
introduces your
child to the
concept of adding
'one more'.

- Start by singing this rhyme:

  'How many creatures went to the zoo?
  Me and you and one more too.
  It ... was ... a ... horse.
  Neigh, neigh, we heard him say.
  How many went to the zoo that day?'

- Put a toy horse on the table and count to three
  (you, your child and the horse).

- Now sing the next verse and add a cow. Keep
  going until you run out of toy animals!

finish that song
from 4 years

The tune and
rhythm of this
nursery rhyme will
prompt your child
to remember
numbers.

- Sing the following rhyme:

  'One, two, three, four, five,
  Once I caught a fish alive.
  Six, seven, eight, nine, ten,
  Then I put him back again!'

- Sing the song again, pausing to allow your child to say
  the numbers five and ten.

- If she finds this easy, let her say more of the numbers,
  or see if she can sing the whole song on her own.

one potato, two potato
from 4 years

This well known playground rhyme gives your child basic counting practice.

- Recite the rhyme below, gently banging one fist on top of the other.

  'One potato, two potato,
  Three potato, four.
  Five potato, six potato,
  Seven potato, more!'

- Make up variations on this rhyme by substituting other three-syllable words for 'potato', such as 'tomato' or 'marshmallow'.

pirate ship
from 4 years

Use this rhyme to teach your child that numbers can reflect a person's age.

- Recite this rhyme and ask your child to act out the captain's lines.

  'When I was one I sucked my thumb
  The day I went to sea. I jumped aboard a pirate ship
  And the captain said to me:
  "We're going this way, that way,
  Forwards and backwards, over the Irish sea.
  A bottle of rum to fill my tum and that's the life for me!"'

- Begin each new verse with a new age. For example:

  'When I was two I buckled my shoe.'
  'When I was three I bumped my knee.'
  'When I was four I opened the door.'
  'When I was five I did a dive.'

five little monkeys

from 3 years

Children love this mischievous song and learn to count down from five as they act it out.

- Find four soft toys and sit them on the floor. Say this rhyme in a bouncy rhythm, inviting your child to join in the actions:

  'Five little monkeys jumping on the bed'
  (bounce up and down)

  'One fell off and bumped his head' (rub your head)

  'We called for the doctor' (pretend to dial)

  'And the doctor said,

  "No more monkeys jumping on the bed!"'
  (wag your finger).

- Take one toy away and repeat the verse with four monkeys. Keep going until you are down to one little monkey (your child) then change the last line to:

  'You're the last little monkey jumping on this bed!'

RESEARCH SAYS

❛ A mnemonic is a device to aid memory. Nursery rhymes that include counting up and down serve as important mnemonics for children who are learning to memorize number order. ❜

stepping stones
from 4 years

This musical game teaches your child that the bigger your steps, the fewer you need to take to get somewhere.

- Tell your child that he's on a magical riverbank. As long as music is playing he is safe. But when the music stops he must cross the river on stepping stones.

- Play some music that he can dance to.

- Stop the music and tell your child to cross the river on three elephant stepping stones, taking giant-sized steps.

- Next time you stop the music he must cross the river on nine small mouse stepping stones. Count them with him.

- Introduce other numbers and sizes of stepping stones, such as five medium-sized fox stepping stones, six small rabbit stepping stones, four big wolf stepping stones, and ten tiny beetle stepping stones. Finish with 12 just-right-sized people stepping stones!

how many?
from 4½ years

This game challenges both your child's physical and counting skills!

- Choose a rhyme that your child knows the words to, such as Twinkle Twinkle Little Star or Humpty Dumpty.

- Sing the song and ask your child to skip. Can he count the number of skips he can do while you are singing the rhyme?

- Now ask him to count the number of hops, jumps, stamps and claps he can do in one rhyme.

- Make a chart together that shows how many of each activity your child did.

on the march

from 3 years

Marching games give your child a regular rhythm to count along to.

- Play some lively music and march around the room counting up to ten.

- As you get to ten, shout out an action for your child to do. Vary the action each time, for example, jump, hop, sit down, turn around, curl in a ball or stretch up tall.

- Make the game more difficult by stopping at a number between one and ten and asking your child to perform an action that number of times.

- Instead of marching, tell your child he must hop until five, then skip until ten. Your child can beat a toy drum in time to his marching.

RESEARCH SAYS

❝ Marching, jumping and skipping helps children to let off steam and get their blood pumping around their body. Children need this kind of physical exertion if they are to settle down, concentrate and learn effectively. ❞

hunt the brick

from 4 years

This hide-and-seek game encourages your child to be aware of different volumes of sound.

- Hide ten small wooden bricks in a room and ask your child to look for them.

- Tell your child that you will help her to find the bricks by shaking a rattle. The nearer she is to a brick, the louder the noise of the rattle; the further away she is, the softer the noise of the rattle.

- You can extend this game by drawing ten bricks on a piece of paper (write the number beside each one) and getting your child to colour each one in as she finds it.

RESEARCH SAYS

❛ A child's awareness of sound can be honed by encouraging her to tune in to the range of sounds in her environment and listen carefully to the subtle differences between sounds. ❜

where am I?

from 4 years

Can your child use logic to work out where you are from the sounds you describe?

- Describe these sounds to your child (or try imitating them) and ask her to guess where you might be.

  'I can hear seagulls above my head and water lapping on sand.'

  'I can hear cows mooing, a cock crowing and a tractor rumbling.'

  'I can hear children laughing, presents being opened and balloons popping.'

  'I can hear bicycle bells and ducks quacking.'

- When you next go to any of these places try standing still with your child and listing all the actual sounds you hear.

sound pairs

from 4 years

This game teaches your child to become sensitive to the differences between sounds.

- Collect six identical plastic bottles. Cover the outsides with paper so that the contents can't be seen.

- Put some salt in two of the bottles, some rice in another two and some dried beans in the last two. Replace the caps securely.

- Mix up the bottles and ask your child to shake each one in turn, then put them together in pairs.

- When she's finished, let her remove the paper to see if she's right.

clap along
from 3 years

Clapping games help to develop a sense of rhythm and can get children used to counting to a beat.

- Sit opposite your child and get used to clapping in time with each other.
- Clap to the count of ten, saying a number out loud each time you clap.
- Clap out the syllables of your child's name. Repeat this several times, saying the name at different speeds.
- Finally, clap out some simple phrases, such as 'teddy has a woolly jumper', and count how many syllables there are in each one.

noisy animals!
from 4 years

This noisy animal game shows your child how to clap in simple rhythms.

- Show your child how to clap three times, pause, clap another three times, pause and so on.
- Now make animal noises in groups of three, for example, 'woof, woof, woof', and ask your child to clap in time.
- Now make animal noises in groups of four and ask him to clap along.
- Swap roles so that your child makes the animal sounds.

musical chit-chat

from 3 years

Having a musical 'conversation' encourages your child to listen very carefully to the number of beats you are playing.

- Find two toy drums – one for you and one for your child. Alternatively, improvise with upturned saucepans.

- Bang one beat on your drum. Ask your child to reply with one beat.

- Beat two times on your drum and ask your child to reply once again.

- Gradually increase the number of beats you want him to copy. Let him play some for you to copy too.

- If your child finds this hard, count the beats out loud as you play them.

RESEARCH SAYS

6 Music and rhythm are naturally comforting to children. Moving in time to music is an important form of non-verbal expression. It helps young children to express feelings that they don't yet have the language skills to vocalize. 9

index

about the authors

Dr Bonnie Macmillan is an educational psychologist. She has 30 years' experience in the field of education, teaching young children, and conducting and analyzing experimental research on reading methods, learning, memory and children's brain development.

Dr Dorothy Einon is the author of a number of bestselling books on early years play. A psychologist at University College, London, with a special interest in child development, Dr Einon has researched the functions of play and the psychology of learning. She has taught in educational centres around the world and appears regularly on television and radio.

Early years specialists and authors **Jane Kemp** and **Clare Walters** provided the activities in *Number and Logic Games*. They have worked with parents and children for many years, both as mothers themselves and as staff on *Practical Parenting* magazine. They have co-authored a number of books for children including *Party Games*, *Travel Games* and *Brain Games for Preschoolers*, all published by Hamlyn.

acknowledgements

Photography © Octopus Publishing
Group Limited /Adrian Pope and
Peter Pugh-Cook.

Executive Editor **Jane McIntosh**
Managing Editor **Clare Churly**
Editorial Assistant **Jennifer Barr**
Design Manager **Tokiko Morishima**
Production Manager **Ian Paton**